GEORGE BARNA
AUTHOR OF MARKETING THE CHURCH

THE
FROG
IN THE
KETTLE

WHAT CHRISTIANS NEED TO KNOW ABOUT LIFE IN THE YEAR 2000

■ WHAT THE FUTURE WILL BE LIKE ■ HOW THE "NEW VALUES" WILL AFFECT THE CHURCH ■ HOW CHRISTIANS NEED TO RESPOND TO THE CHANGING ENVIRONMENT

Regal Books

A Division of Gospel Light
Ventura, California, U.S.A.

Published by Regal Books
A Division of GL Publications
Ventura, California 93006
Printed in U.S.A.

Library of Congress Cataloging-in-Publication Data
Barna, George.
        The frog in the kettle : what the Christian community needs to
know about life in the year 2000 / George Barna.
        p.   cm.
        ISBN 0-8307-1449-9
        1. Christianity—United States. 2. Twenty-first century—Forecasts.
3. United States—Church history.   I. Title.
BR526.B36 1990
201'.12—dc20   90-37367
                                                                    CIP

    2 3 4 5 6 7 8 9 10 /X/KP/ 94 93 92 91 90

Rights for publishing this book in other languages are contracted by Gospel
Literature International (GLINT) foundation. GLINT also provides technical
help for the adaptation, translation, and publishing of Bible study resources
and books in scores of languages worldwide. For further information, contact
GLINT, Post Office Box 488, Rosemead, California, 91770, U.S.A., or the pub-
lisher.

ACKNOWLEDGMENTS

ALTHOUGH MY NAME APPEARS AS THE AUTHOR OF THIS BOOK, many friends, colleagues and family members have also helped it see the light of day. Their prayers, words of encouragement and substantive assistance have been invaluable.

The staff at Barna Research have been understanding during times when I was absent in order to reflect and to write. I am pleased to work with these professionals, and to share their commitment to the Church. My heartfelt thanks to Cindy Fiori, Keith Lindstrom, Paul Rottler, Ron Sellers and Jim Stipe. It is my prayer that this book will be a work of which they will be proud, since much of the data referred to in these pages has been collected and analyzed in partnership with them. May this be one of a series of communications we produce that will reach the Church and produce favorable results.

Various friends and associates have been a source of strength and insight throughout the process. Especially helpful have been Greg Roth and Jack Hardgrave, who offered moral support during pressure periods; and Larry Linamen, whose advice and friendship have greatly helped me in this endeavor.

My cohorts at Regal Books have also been crucial in this project. Ron Durham edited the book with a keen eye to making a dry subject more lively. Bill Greig III has consistently been a cheerleader for this book and for our work in general. His support has inspired me to commit the type of energy and effort required to make this book a serious challenge to the

Church that we both love so much. Mark Maddox has also been a positive force in the development of the project. I am grateful to work with a Christian publishing company that is setting its sights on the future, in the hope of serving Christ as effectively as possible.

As always, my most important reality check and source of encouragement has been my wife, Nancy. She has believed in me and in the ministry of our company from the start. During the trials and tribulations we have faced, she has been a voice of love and understanding. Her reading of many drafts of these chapters was instrumental in the shaping and reshaping of the content. She has been a capable and valued partner in ministry and in life. I am eternally grateful to God for bringing us together, and for her support through our various projects.

Finally, I am grateful to God for providing me a forum for sharing information with His people. I pray that this book will be used by those who know Him and love Him, toward guiding the Church to better health and impact in America. These are treacherous times. Please be aware of and responsive to the challenges and opportunities that we have to influence a dying world for the glory of the God who created us, and the Son who saved us.

CONTENTS

A DAY IN THE LIFE OF JILL: MAY 17, 2000

Meet Jill.

A single parent in her early 40s, Jill and her son, Jackson, live in a large apartment complex in Dallas, Texas. Jackson is in the eighth grade at the local public junior high school. They have lived there for nearly two years, although Jill is always on the lookout for a better living situation.

Jill works at a nearby insurance company as a service representative supervisor. She is responsible for managing a staff of people, mostly women, who maintain computerized records of claims. She has worked there for four years, making her one of the senior staff people. She is also the only Caucasian in the group.

The insistent buzz of her alarm clock awakens Jill at 7:30 A.M. As always, her first fuzzy mental act is to think of a good reason to get up today. Then she remembers: at least today is Friday, and payday. She shakes Jackson awake, showers and enters the kitchen to make breakfast. In the background, the morning television news program sets the tone for the day.

Jackson breezes in, stops at the breakfast bar just long enough to toss down a glass of orange juice, then dashes off to catch the bus to school. Jill shouts at him as he disappears through the door, informing him that she will not be home until late that evening, and that he should make his own dinner whenever he's hungry. Used to the routine, Jackson nods in acknowledgment as he goes out the door.

Although she would like to linger over a second cup of coffee, Jill rouses herself from her chair when the kitchen clock warns her that it's time to get ready for work. Reluctantly she forces herself to focus on the day ahead. She is bored with her job, and with the people with whom she works, but what's a working woman to do?

When she returns to the bedroom to get dressed for work, Jill unintentionally awakens Bob, her current live-in companion. He grumbles incoherently and turns over for another few winks. Bob works on a flex-time schedule and is under no pressure to be in the office by 9 o'clock. It's the kind of schedule Jill envies. Any new job, though, would have to match her existing benefits package. Even more importantly, she treasures the ability to mentally leave the job behind come 5 P.M. Her job is important, but she knows she will never make it to the executive ranks. She is stuck in a limited-mobility position, and any real fulfillment she gets out of life will have to come from something other than her work.

After putting on the finishing touches to her makeup, Jill rushes to the parking lot, starts her flashy red sports coupe and begins the slow drive to work. The traffic is clogging the streets as usual. It takes her 30 minutes to travel the six miles to her office building, and 10 more minutes to make the trek from the 11th floor of the parking garage to her office. Once inside, she nods a silent greeting to the few coworkers there and logs on to her computer. This will be her world for the next seven hours, as she generates reports and monitors the entries of her employees.

The job has become so routine for Jill that her mind frequently wanders while she stares at the display screen in front of her. Since her company closed its large downtown office in favor of setting up smaller, less expensive satellite offices, she has fewer contacts with people her own age, and has felt more isolated. It's so hard to meet people in the city! And even when she does, it seems that they are becoming harder and harder to really get to know. Even when you meet someone you like, trying to connect with them again is virtually impossible. Everyone is so busy. And everyone is so guarded, afraid of being taken advantage of.

Jill tries not to let the hollowness inside get the best of her, but she can feel it gnawing away, down deep. Yes, she has the sports car, stylish clothing and the latest in home entertainment equipment. But none of it fills the hollow place, and she is almost desperately lonely. Her divorce was relatively amicable, but it left her feeling like a failure. Her psychologist consistently tried to impress upon her that such feelings were normal. In today's society, he told her, she would be abnormal only if she did *not* experience at least one broken marriage during her lifetime. Even so, the experience gave new meaning to the term "broken." Raising Jackson was not easy, although he pretty much looked after himself. Then, too, she felt frustrated that despite her $52,000 annual salary it was increasingly difficult to make ends meet. What she wouldn't give for another $10,000 a year to ease some of the financial stress.

Friday nights were her only break from the dull routine. Tonight she plans to go to the local YWCA for an aerobics class and a game of racquetball. Afterwards she will meet Bob for dinner at their favorite restaurant, and they will probably follow that with drinks and a movie, or some other diversion. And maybe something unexpected would come up to relieve the pressures and responsibilities and the deadly sameness of Jill's world.

Payday—the best part about Fridays. Perhaps this pay period

Jill will be able to stow away another $25 or so toward that tailored suit she had seen advertised on the cable shopping channel recently. And the usual $50 per paycheck will get stashed in her vacation fund. But how will she ever get ahead enough to get some of those new kitchen conveniences and car accessories that have been on the market for almost a year? And what about Jackson's plea for the new computer software he needs to help him do better on his homework assignments?

Before leaving the office at the end of the day, Jill quickly phones Jackson to be sure he's all right. She scowls and slams down the receiver when all she hears is her own voice, courtesy of their answering machine. Where would that rascal Jackson be at this time of day? With street gangs everywhere, widespread drug use, legalized gambling and the sexual opportunities available to kids these days, she often wonders if she would give birth to a child today, given the opportunity to make that decision.

Suddenly Jill remembers a commitment she had made to ACME—the Association for the Containment of Medical Expenses, a volunteer group she supports. She hurriedly dials their number, then punches in the extension of her contact there. Once connected, Jill explains, to the chagrin of the volunteer director, that she simply can't help tonight with the fund-raising dinner that had been planned for three months, as she had promised. When the volunteer director asks how ACME could possibly find someone to replace Jill at this late hour, Jill suggests that the director simply divide her responsibilities among the others who would be there. Frowning again, Jill shakes her head as she hangs up the telephone. How could her absence create such concern? And what right does the volunteer director have to make her feel guilty? Last minute cancellations happen all the time, she reasons.

On her way to the Y, she passes by building after steel and glass building, without noticing the seven or eight churches among them. She isn't even aware they exist. It's been two or three years since Jill has been to a church service, other than Uncle Wayne's funeral last year, and the Easter service she attended with her mother during her visit two years ago. Sundays are her day to sleep in, and to get in some serious relaxation. Besides, nobody attends church these days. If pressed, Jill would have described the Church as an outdated, declining institution. Sure, there is probably a God, she would have argued. But religious beliefs are a private matter. She has her own beliefs—that all people can dictate their own destiny, that love is important, that the Golden Rule is the core of a successful society, that because there is no life after death what we do in the here-and-now is all that's real. No need to belong to some group of old ladies singing irrelevant hymns to a droning organ, sitting in uncomfortable pews and listening to a judgmental treatise on some finer point of theology that has nothing to do with paying this month's rent, keeping Jackson off drugs or repairing her fractured self-esteem.

Bob meets Jill for dinner after her workout at the Y. The restaurant, as is typical on Friday evenings, is jammed. After their meal they crawl for 20 minutes in the freeway traffic before exiting to see a movie at the mall. Tired from a seemingly endless week, they decide to forego the post-movie dessert and drinks, and head home instead.

Although it's nearly 11 P.M., Jackson is still up, playing a computer game in his room, while a rented video movie plays on the TV in the living room. He is full of news about his day, and the grocery shopping he did for the household. After listening wearily to his outburst for 10 minutes, Jill insists that he go to bed. He is so tired he doesn't protest, even wishing Jill and Bob good night. But after closing the door to his bedroom he turns on a movie on one of the pay channels before going to bed.

Fatigued, Jill and Bob go to bed, too. The excitement she had hoped for hadn't enlivened her life today.

Maybe tomorrow. . . .

PART I SHAPING TOMORROW TODAY

Charged by Christ Himself to be agents to change the world rather than agents changed by the world, we have been mesmerized by the lures of modern culture.

1 THE IMPORTANCE OF ANTICIPATING THE FUTURE

CHAPTER HIGHLIGHTS:

▶Christians have a responsibility to respond intelligently to the world around them.
▶England: a living example of the effects of secularism. America is following in the same footsteps.

▶The '90s will bring significant changes in values, beliefs, life-styles and opportunities. How will the Church respond?

 ▶▶▶▶▶

THIS IS NOT JUST ANOTHER FUTURIST BOOK WITH MORE PREDICTIONS about technological breakthroughs, cultural transformations, shifts in attitudes and economic turbulence. Such books are important, for there is no doubt about it: life is changing, and the past is, well, history. We are moving—or being moved—to new horizons.

This book is more about Jill, whom you met in the Prologue, and about the millions of others like her who will inhabit the world that the futurist books describe. It is about the changes in approach and the new awareness to which God is calling His people in order to connect with the Jills of tomorrow.

Why worry about what might happen tomorrow, when, we could be concentrating upon the difficulties of today, instead? After all, didn't Jesus warn against worrying about the future in the Sermon on the Mount? Isn't it the responsibility of a Christian to avoid anxiety about tomorrow, and focus on the opportunities of today?[1]

Of course it is wrong to dwell on the future to the neglect of the work we've been given to do today. We are responsible for making the most of existing realities, rather than aimlessly daydreaming about what might happen in the years ahead. We must faithfully use our gifts in the situations in which God placed us.

However, Jesus was not teaching us to be unprepared for the future. He was warning against being obsessed with and anxious about the future. Nowhere does the Bible tell us that we are to avoid preparing for the days ahead. Indeed, our duty is to be wise in the ways of the world. We are not to adopt those ways as our own, but to be sensitive enough to them to penetrate the world with the gospel, and to have a ready defense against opposition to the message of Christ. We are supposed to focus upon the future with faith that He is Lord of the future, rather than fearing tomorrow because we lack faith that He will see us through.

When God provides us with opportunities to foresee how to meet Jill's needs—when He gives us glimpses of the future—it is to enable us to serve Him better not only in the future but by making smarter choices today.[2] Do we have the right to dismiss such signs of the times, their potential for today and their implications for tomorrow? Is it a Christian virtue to ignore God's handwriting on the wall?

OF FROGS AND BRITONS AND THE DANGER OF GRADUALISM

The signs we need to perceive are not vague predictions about the future—many are present realities. The trouble is that they occur so gradually that we often do not notice them. It's like the familiar story of the frog and the kettle of water. Place a frog in boiling water and it will jump out immediately because it can tell that it's in a hostile environment. But place a frog in a kettle of room-temperature water and it will stay there, content with those surroundings. Slowly, very slowly, increase the temperature of the water. This time, the frog doesn't leap out, but just stays there, unaware that the environment is changing. Continue to turn up the burner until the water is boiling. Our poor frog will be boiled, too—quite content, perhaps, but nevertheless dead.

The Christian community in America might be expected to be more aware of current changes in the environment than the frog in the kettle. Yet, for the past two decades, at least, the Church has been generally insensitive to those changes. We have continued to operate as though our environment has remained the same. Like the frog, we are faced with the very real possibility of dying because of our unresponsiveness to the changing world around us.

The Example on Our Doorstep

This insensitivity is all the more remarkable because we have an opportunity to observe the very process that threatens us. It has occurred in recent times almost on our doorstep. Many Christians in England warn that we are undergoing in this country a rise in the "temperature" of our spiritual environment much like they experienced in their own land.

These observers recall when England was a nation in which the Church was the central institution of society. Moral values, social behavior, cultural activities, family development, lifestyles and even political decision-making all revolved around the nation's religious perspective and spiritual sensitivity. Ingrained in the nation's thinking was the belief that the highest goal in life is to worship and serve God.

More recently these values have been undermined by the encroachment of secularism. There is more concern now for the material than for the spiritual. God is no longer at the center of the nation's agenda. Its Christian community has all but disappeared. Once representing the vast majority of that great nation's population, true believers are estimated now to be only about 2 percent of the population.

There are striking similarities between the spiritual decline of England and the current spiritual condition of the United States. A thoughtful evaluation of modern America—our social, political, spiritual, moral and economic condition—shows how insidiously our own spiritual foundations are deteriorating. We, too, are a materialistic society, more concerned about the physical comforts of today than the spiritual needs of the future. It is very hard to persuade us to think seriously about the effects of cultural change on the nation's religious beliefs and behavior.

Mesmerized—and Losing Ground

The result is that the Christian community, in the midst of a whirlpool of change and a hostile societal environment, is losing the battle. Charged by Christ Himself to be agents to change the world rather than agents changed by the world, we

---

Nowhere does the Bible tell us that we are to avoid preparing for the days ahead. Indeed, our duty is to be wise in the ways of the world.

---

have been mesmerized by the lures of modern culture. Rather than prepare for the coming battles, we revel in past victories, focusing on what can never be changed or relived, at the expense of tomorrow's opportunities.

Consequently, America in the '90s is rotting from the inside out. We are suffering from constant, if almost imperceptible, shifts in perspective and behavior. As our population matures in technological sophistication and material comfort, we are losing our spiritual edge. We have embraced the means rather than the ends. Service to God has been replaced by a thirst for exaltation of self.

THE ONLY CONSTANT IS THE SLOW DRIP OF CONSTANT CHANGE

Change is now a constant in America. Some changes, such as the transformations in Eastern Europe and the Soviet Union, seem to happen overnight. Fax machines were embraced by businesses within a couple of years after they were first introduced. Video rentals for home use passed theatre revenues within only a few years. The Reagan presidency suddenly made it fashionable to be conservative after two decades of liberalism.

Most changes, however, are less immediate. In fact, what makes most social change today so disarming is that it is more *evolutionary* than *revolutionary*. Each day brings an incremental shift in some fundamental aspect of life, a small ripple that we often overlook because we are on guard only for tidal waves. Anxiously awaiting major overhauls of our perspectives and experiences, we tend to dismiss the minute, tiny adjustments going on about us as insignificant. We have missed the fact that the cumulative effect of these minor alterations has resulted in changes in our world that in reality are far greater than the single, big bang that we have been so steadfastly awaiting. What is happening is more like Chinese water torture, with the water slowly eroding, one drip at a time, the foundations of our Christian culture.

Social scientists tell us that if we could stand back and measure the rate of change in modern America, we would discover that things are changing at a faster pace than ever before. But not many of us ever take the time to gain the big picture. Immersed in a daily struggle for survival, and stimulated by the possibility of prosperity and happiness, we plant ourselves in the short term. Thus, the numerous changes that are reshaping our everyday reality go unnoticed and unanswered.

WILL CHANGE MAKE US NUMB IN THE '90S?

People talk about how different things were in the '80s, and how time seemed to whiz by at breakneck speed. They haven't seen anything yet. Before we reach the turn of the century, the present decade will bring countless changes, including the following.

■ *Values.* We will become even more self-centered, more materialistic, more driven to play. While we will value relationships, most of us will be too selfish to make the hard commitments and sacrifices that facilitate any meaningful relationships.

■ *Currency.* Time will replace money as tomorrow's currency of choice. We will be able to obtain the almighty dollar more readily than the necessary minutes in which to cram everything we want to do in each hectic day.

■ *Beliefs.* Many people already feel that nobody knows what they need better than they do—including God, or any other spiritual entity. In the '90s we will develop more blends of pop religion. Our choice of a religious system, however, will be based on that system's ability to satisfy our own personal needs and desires. Religion will be viewed as less of a corporate experience, and more of a self-fulfilling process. These personalized religious systems will satiate our need for a religious perspective, without requiring the sacrifice and commitments that some faiths, like Christianity, demand.

■ *Background.* Gone are the days of America as the young, white, middle-class nation. By the year 2000, Americans will be darker, more wrinkled and from more widely divergent economic backgrounds. An entirely new class system is emerging, in which the traditional "haves" may lose their economic and social standing.

■ *Tools.* Americans will openly embrace technology in the '90s, as we shift from an emphasis on innovation to an emphasis on application. The result will be increasing acceptance of technology as a means to an end, bringing new attitudes and life-styles into being.

■ *Institutions.* The local church will have to earn its place in people's hearts. Institutional loyalty, the presumption of their credibility and altruistic support of them will largely disappear. Only if the institution provides high quality benefits to the individual will it stand a chance of gaining attention and support.

All of this means that the traditions and understandings many Christians have grown up with are being replaced, and a new series of realities are being ushered in. Even though the changes are minute and incremental, we need not be anesthetized against being aware that their cumulative effect will be comprehensive turbulence in our entire society.

A PIVOTAL DECADE IN THE HISTORY OF THE FAITH

What a tremendous opportunity the Christian community has to influence lives during this period! As Americans struggle to make sense of their new environment, the Body of Christ has the chance to offer real, practical, biblical solutions to our nation.

However, the old approaches and traditional strategies for sharing our faith will no longer work in the '90s. We have to be clever enough to analyze our environment and provide creative responses to the challenges we face.

Make no mistake about it: the pressure on the Christian community is mounting. Typically, we have been five to ten years behind society, responding to changing conditions long after transitions have begun. And now we have run out of time. If we want the Christian faith to remain a vibrant alternative to the world system, we must stop *reacting* and start *anticipating*.

The '90s are a pivotal decade in the history of American Christianity. It is a time in which the Church will either explode with new growth or quietly fade into a colorless thread in the fabric of a secular culture. The changing nature of our society has pushed us past the point of simply being able to mark time. In this decade, Christianity must prove itself to be real and viable, or become just another spiritual philosophy appearing in the history of mankind.

Effective ministry in the years ahead will be quite different from meaningful ministry today. In fact, it is likely that ministry in the year 2000 will be as different from ministry in 1980, as ministry in 1980 was from ministry in 1900. Change is occurring that quickly. And we must develop intelligent and effective responses, in service to Christ, just as rapidly.

Effective, or Affected?

Identifying trends and preparing to address the future will enable us to keep pace with a secularized society that is bent on wringing all the self-serving benefits it can from the current transformation of our nation. By being forward-looking in our thinking, we can become effective change agents, rather than affected changed agents.

In the chapters that follow, you will read about the America of the early '90s, and the America of the year 2000. As you read, remember that we are not describing our existing state and our prospective future merely to satisfy curiosity, or for sheer entertainment. Our aim is to better arm you for the raging spiritual battles ahead with pertinent information and a realistic perspective. Our goal as the Christian community must be to save society from itself. The objective of this book is to help you to perceive the condition of the world, and the outcomes toward which we are careening. Unless we acknowledge where we are headed and develop insightful strategies for redirecting the nation's path, we will find the church to be just another ineffective if well-intentioned institution.

Keep in mind Paul's exhortation that we must be sensitive to our culture, adapting our approaches without compromising

our message.[3] America's superficial spirituality demands that
we rededicate ourselves to proclaiming the gospel in new ways
that are relevant to people's lives. The skin-deep commitment
of most Christians to their faith requires that we first get our
own house in order before we can hope to present a strong and
attractive witness to a watching and skeptical world. Our environment now dictates that we shake loose the outdated
assumptions we have about people's character, and provide
this culture with a realistic and enticing alternative to materialism and selfishness.

In the chapters that follow, I pray that you will be stimulated to rethink your personal ministry and how you and your
church can become more effective at reaching the lost and the
nominally religious. We have an enormously difficult yet
potentially productive challenge in the decade ahead. May the
information and perspective in this book enable you to
respond with enthusiasm to that challenge for the glory of
Christ.

Notes
1. Matt. 6:25-34.
2. Luke 14:28-30.
3. 1 Cor. 9:19-23.

PART II

CHANGES IN BEHAVIOR AND LIFE-STYLE

It will be increasingly difficult to convince the unchurched that our faith is pertinent to the 21st century if the tools of our trade are from the last century.

2 DEMANDS THAT WILL AFFECT OUR VALUES

CHAPTER HIGHLIGHTS:

▶The gradual changes of the '90s—the result of three decades of ferment—will hit with full force by 2000.

▶Today's values—affluence, self, short-term commitments and quality; tomorrow's skepticism about other people and institutions, suspicious of traditions.

▶The "mores" of tomorrow: more accepting of change; more protective of our time; more devoted to gaining control over our life, more interested in being accepted as a unique individual.

▶Tomorrow's agenda for the Church: reassess the role and use of traditions, the quality of ministry, sensitivity to people's time.

▶As life-styles and expectations change, so must our definitions of the Church's success and growth. Membership figures will be less meaningful.

▶Overt integrity: a central element to successful ministry in the '90s.

Much OF THE CHANGE THAT WILL AFFECT OUR LIVES IN THE NEW century will be the result of fundamental transformations in what we expect from life, and what we consider to be important and valuable. While the '60s broke through the barriers to change in these areas, the '90s will bring renewed energy to the process of redefining our basic values and assumptions about life. Some of the transitions begun in the '80s will come to fruition in this decade, as we radically revise our understanding of what is possible, what is necessary and what is worthwhile.

Our values and expectations impact every decision we make during the day. They serve as the filter through which we interpret our world, and determine how we respond to our surroundings. As we continue to challenge assumptions about who we are and what we want, the result is a unique and constantly changing understanding about good and bad, desirable and despicable, worthwhile and worthless, important and insignificant.

AMERICA, 1990

As we enter the '90s, the way we look at life is already in a state of flux. Our values have undergone a continuing series of shifts since the '60s made it acceptable to challenge tradition and the status quo. Once the social revolution of that era launched the reexamination of even our most basic moral and social rules, we have constantly explored new avenues of change in our value systems. We have tentatively experimented with new values and their resulting behaviors, and either accepted or rejected those forms after a trial period.

Our Changing Values

We used to value:	*We are going to value:*
Quantity of possessions	Quality of possessions
Money	Time
Old traditions	New traditions
Commitment	Flexibility
Group identity	Individualism
Trusting people	Proven integrity
Satisfaction through work	Satisfaction through leisure

Materialism Is In

The desire to be affluent still motivates much of our activity. Although raised in relative opulence, "the Boomer" generation—Americans born in the "baby boom" between 1946 and 1964—still aspires to have more than even their parents achieved. But the *attitudes* toward affluence differ greatly between the generations. Parents of Boomers were driven to achieve status and wealth, because it was a challenge. Boomers are driven to achieve because they are accustomed to the good life, and see continued comfort as their right.

Our actions on the job, in the marketplace, with our families and in our free time are greatly impacted by the desire to possess things. Materialism, despite the bad rap it has received from the press and from the Christian community, continues to rule the minds and hearts of Americans.

Commitment Is Out

In the process of redefining what counts in life, many of us have decided that commitment is not in our best interests. Tra-

Signs of Reduced Commitments in Life

■ Divorce rate is climbing: half of all new marriages will end in divorce.

■ Adults feel they have fewer close friends than did adults in past decades.

■ Brand loyalty in consumer purchasing studies has dropped in most product categories, and by as much as 60 percent in some categories.

■ Proportion of people willing to join an organization as a formal member is declining in relation to churches, labor unions, political parties and clubs, and community improvement associations.

■ Book clubs and record clubs were unable to attract new members when multiple-year or multi-product commitments were required; revenues have increased greatly upon removing long-term commitment demands.

■ Percentage of adults who consider it their duty to fight for their country, regardless of the cause, has dropped.

■ Percentage of people who commit to attending events but fail to show is on the rise.

■ Parents are less likely to believe that it is important to remain in an unhappy marriage for the sake of the children than they were 20 years ago.

ditional concepts such as loyalty and the importance of membership in various groups have been thrown out in favor of personal interest and self-preservation. Notice that book clubs and record clubs no longer ask people to make long-term commitments—a marked change in the way they market their products. Church membership figures have been declining for the past decade because people are not willing to restrict themselves by such commitments. Marriage, the most traditional of our society's long-term commitments, is being realigned through divorce and other forms of family.

Commitment is viewed negatively because it limits our ability to feel independent and free, to experience new things, to change our minds on the spur of the moment and to focus upon self-gratification rather than helping others. People willingly make commitments only when the expected outcome exceeds what they must sacrifice as a result of that commitment.

The Quest for the Best

America has also been intrigued by the concept of excellence. For the past decade, we have stressed the importance of providing quality in products and services. As consumers, we strive to locate companies that are dedicated to excellence as manifested through product quality and customer service. As employees, we are most interested in working for organizations whose performance is tops, and which esteem competence.

At the same time, we are looking not only for quality in performance, but quality in character—the moral and ethical dimension. Think about the behavioral standards we expect of congressmen and presidential candidates—standards that few of us would be able to live up to. We also hold employers, corporations, religious leaders and others in positions of authority and influence to tougher standards than we would satisfy.

Again, the "me first" mindset is evident: we believe that

because we are unique and affluent, we deserve the best. Any person or institution that can provide us with the best is acceptable—although we will not make any long-term commitments to them.

Skepticism Rules
Part of this short-term mentality is a reflection of our deeply-imbedded skepticism. In the past decade or so, we have encountered revelations about treacherous behavior by our political leaders; public deceit by popular television ministries; fraud perpetrated against innocent people by leading financial institutions and advisers; and increasing abuse of the truth by advertisers in the mass media. While our judicial system is based on the principle of "innocent until proven guilty," the population at-large lives by the rule, "guilty until proven innocent." Americans are deathly afraid of being taken advantage of—largely because we have been taken advantage of so often by people and organizations we have trusted in the past.

Traditions? Why?
A related outcome is the reduced respect we have for tradition. Whether we look at our schools, our churches, our families or any other important institution or convention in life, we have largely decided that the past is gone, and that tradition must go with it. Nowadays traditions last only if they can be proved relevant and superior to other options. Given the widespread acceptance of the '60s philosophy that you can do whatever works best for you as long as it does not harm someone else, traditions are seen as limitations and restrictions. They may be seen as a starting point rather than an ending point; or as a point of information rather than a guiding principle.

Among the traditions we have cast aside are those related to life-style and gender roles. Men are increasingly responsible for family care: housework, child care, social developments. Women have assumed more responsibility related to providing income, handling family legal and accounting matters, attaining education and accepting decision-making positions within the church and other organizations. The lines of responsibility have been blurred to the point that it is difficult to identify "a man's job" any more—and even when we try we run the risk of being branded "sexist" or "out-of-touch."

Rather than accept limitations in life-style, we will rewrite the rules of the game.

AMERICA, 2000

The '90s will support the continuing revision of our values and expectations related to people and institutions. Rather than creating wildly new ways of life, however, we will design a new value system that is a synthesis of old and new concepts. This will provide incremental changes that combine some of the comfort and stability of the old, known ways with the excitement, relevance and freedom of a new approach.

No More "Satisficing"
More than ever, Americans in the '90s will refuse to settle for anything less than exactly what they want. In the '70s, sociologists coined the term "satisficing" to describe our willingness to sacrifice some desires in order to achieve the optimal mix of possibilities. By 2000, satisficing will be viewed as a defeatist

philosophy, the mark of a person too weak or too unresourceful to get what is desired or deserved. Rather than accept limitations in life-style, we will rewrite the rules of the game. Having experienced the ability to restructure our daily situations to better suit our needs, fewer and fewer adults will allow "the way it is" to determine "the way it should be."

Redefining Change

This boldness is an outgrowth of the way Baby Boomers and Baby Busters (the generation after the Boomers) have redefined change. To the parents of Boomers, change was a risk; it threatened what they had achieved. But to Boomers and Busters, change represents an opportunity, the best avenue to new possibilities and breakthroughs. The willingness to accept change is viewed as a sign of health; resistance to change, without a strong rationale, is seen as short-sighted and foolish. While many of us still find too much change happening too quickly to be emotionally unsettling, the lust to experience life more expansively will entice more and more of us to discard doubts and fears regarding change.

The Best, if Not the Most

While we may not settle for anything less than the best we feel we deserve, we will also become a somewhat less acquisition-crazed culture. The '70s and '80s were described as decades of "conspicuous consumption." The '90s may become a time of "critical consumption," in which we are not interested in having a lot of stuff—just the best stuff. We are shifting from an emphasis on quantity to an emphasis on quality. Having failed to achieve satisfaction through possessing *more*, we will seek it through possessing *the best*. This is not a sign of maturity. We will not surrender our desire to possess and experience the good things in life; we simply will not be as diligent about having everything that is available, just for the sake of having everything.

Time: the New "Money"

Perhaps the most significant change will be the new currency we utilize for determining what is of value to us. For several thousand years, mankind has used money as the primary means of establishing value. While money will continue to play a major role in our decisions and actions, by 2000 we will have shifted to using *time* as our dominant indicator of value.

Time is the one resource which we cannot manufacture. It is a non-renewable resource which limits our ability to experience all that we can. In a culture as wealthy as ours, there is no scarcity of money; but every day we feel the frustration of not having enough time to do all the things we desire. In the '90s, more and more of us will pay to protect our time. That is, money will be used to guard the more valuable commodity, time.

We will also find that businesses which save us time and make life convenient will prosper. The '80s brought the VCR, the microwave oven, automatic teller machines, Federal Express, fax machines, home delivery and 24-hour convenience stores. In the '90s, there will be an expansion of such products and services, geared to allowing people the greatest flexibility with their time, and the highest productivity for each minute.

Companies will respond by offering flex-time policies to their employees; stores and banks will extend their hours; more services will be offered at your location rather than a centralized location—services such as auto maintenance, computer repairs and haircuts. Even though some of these conveniences will cost more, cost is not the issue. Thus, although money will not be replaced in our economic system, it will be transcended in our minds and behavior by the importance and limited availability of time.

Come in, Control

During the '90s, in spite of our enjoyment of and desire for possessions and wealth, we will come to believe that success is not about acquisition. It is about *control*. With our schedules increasingly hectic; the economy moving ahead in unforeseen ways, at breakneck speed; relationships coming and going; and with technology altering how we experience reality, life will often seem out of control. Thus, the person who can put the pieces together in such a way as to make sense out of this fast-paced, non-conventional way of life will be seen as successful.

In this process of trying to comprehend and handle the world around us, we will demand elements which provide us with control. In decision-making situations, we will want to know all the options available. Woe to the person who seeks to limit our options, even if the intent is to simplify the possibilities for our benefit. Allowing others to make such decisions for us robs us of control. Skeptics that we are, allowing others (except a trusted few) to do so is not likely.

In the '70s and '80s, Boomers were acclaimed for their extraordinary levels of self-absorption. With the maturing of the Boomers, that self-centeredness will be softened to some extent by a greater interest in community needs. (The self-interest of Boomers will not disappear; it will simply be joined to a heightened sensitivity to the needs of others with whom they have contact.) Although some involvement in community problems will be born from a desire to improve one's own life (e.g. attacking air pollution for better personal health, assisting the homeless to reduce anxiety about personal safety), the fact is that people will show a willingness to commit their time only to a small number of very carefully selected community services.

We will also see a renewed interest in life-styles that provide us with more control. Privacy will be critical to us in the '90s. Unlisted telephone numbers and machines which screen our telephone calls will proliferate. More communities will begin

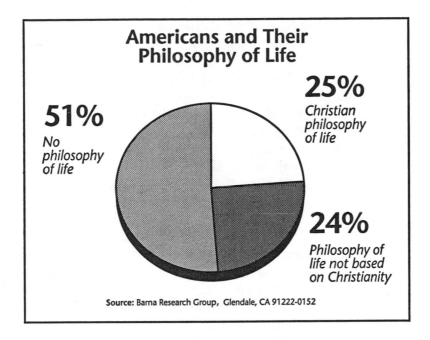

Americans and Their Philosophy of Life

25%
Christian philosophy of life

51%
No philosophy of life

24%
Philosophy of life not based on Christianity

Source: Barna Research Group, Glendale, CA 91222-0152

to regulate door-to-door solicitation. State governments will legislate limitations on telemarketing. Increasing numbers of consumers will request that their names be removed from mailing lists. Participation in public opinion surveys will decline. We will be more cautious about how we release information about ourselves, our families and what we do with our resources.

Varied and Unique
Americans will continue to seek more and more varied experiences. Variety in life-style will be the rage in the '90s, as we experiment with new household styles, novel religious philosophies, unusual occupations and new leisure activities.

Individualism will be exalted. Whereas conformity was a cherished life-style in the past, uniqueness will gain favor in the '90s. We will be very self-conscious, acutely aware of our image to others, but we will consider that image acceptable if it depicts us as "being our own person." Self-expression through styles of clothing, hair styles and colors, and choice of music, will be widespread.

Rather than associate with established groups or philosophies, people will walk the middle ground between different groups, with more of us refusing to affiliate with any one. For instance, people will not label themselves "conservative" or "liberal" since they believe they are both. They will reject the constraints posed by saying they are "Protestant," choosing instead to call themselves "Christian" or "religious." Living according to a particular philosophy of life will lose popularity, in favor of spontaneous response to circumstances and opportunities. No longer shackled by the limitations of relational commitments, we will find it easier than ever to be one-of-a-kind. Individualism will feed our desire for control and our interest in a variety of experiences.

Flexible Traditions

After two decades of tearing down the old traditions, Boomers will search for roots and stability in life, and begin to develop a new set of traditions that they can embrace as their own. Events, awards, organizational practices, family activities—all will witness something of a revival, and will form the new traditions of the 21st century. These traditions, however, will also contain an element of flexibility uncommon to the traditions of old. Boomers and Busters in particular still will not tolerate unbending rules.

For those who value the classic, high-energy "hustle" typical of post-World War II Americans, one of the most disheartening trends relates to the behavior of the Busters. These young adults (born from 1964-1977) have been weaned on success, wealth and comfort. As they mature into adulthood and family responsibilities, they will suffer from having been raised in such easy circumstances. Already, our studies show them to be cut from a different cloth than their predecessors. Although they will retain the high expectations of those who came before them, they lack the same energy and aggressiveness. They will not be trailblazers, nor will they exhibit the same standards for self-performance.

As Busters become a more important part of the national decision-making body, their "laid-back" approach to life will help to slow the pace of change in America, and lead to a reexamination of where we have been and where we are going. After we enter the 21st century, the very success that enabled Busters to live in prosperity and comfort will be a key element that will cause Americans to stop and reevaluate their priorities.

✝ CHALLENGES AND OPPORTUNITIES FOR THE CHURCH

As you read about what we are becoming, it must be obvious that for the Church to continue to do business in the same ways we have for the past 200 years would spell certain decline. Although we may not be cheerful about some of the changes that are likely to occur, we must adapt our forms of outreach to our culture and provide a meaningful experience within the boundaries of that culture.

Reshaping Tradition
Denominational churches that cling to centuries-old traditions may have the toughest time in the '90s. Younger adults are increasingly impatient with organizations that maintain old traditions for the sake of tradition. If your church uses traditional practices or elements—hymns, robes, liturgical language, ritual—it will be urgent to convey the meaning behind those

traditions, and why they are an important part of the life of your church. Do not make assumptions about people's interest in traditional practices. Instead, explore ways of educating them about those traditions which are most critical and will not be changed. Be neither surprised nor offended when many people reject those traditions as antiquated and irrelevant.

Also, realize that we are living in an era in which new traditions can be developed and integrated into the Church. They may bear little or no resemblance to the traditions of the past, but they will enable today's adults to embrace the Church by owning those new forms and concepts. Helping the congregation to shape these new traditions—special songs, seasonal programs, symbols, language—may prove to be one of the integral steps toward attracting newcomers, and retaining many who have lived on the periphery of the spiritual life of the Body.

Quality over Quantity

Local churches must take a hard look at their performance and dedicate themselves to excellence in all they do. In today's marketplace, people are critical and unforgiving. They have high expectations, and they give an organization only one chance to impress. In this type of environment, a church would be better off doing a few things with excellence than many things merely adequately.

Adults desire diversity so they can have the choices and make their own decisions. But if providing diversity undermines the quality of output, the best bet would be to provide fewer options, but higher standards. If the church does not have to make such an either/or choice, it should provide people with options. Allow them to select from more than one Sunday School class. Provide different options for their giving to the church. Let them make the decisions.

Church activities should be structured as conveniently as possible. Provide child care as needed. Have plenty of available parking, with special areas for visitors. Attend to the mobility limitations of the elderly (e.g. selecting room locations requiring fewer stairs to negotiate, special parking closer to the church). Design the bulletins for use in services so they are not cluttered, but are focused on the service and easy to read.

If providing diversity undermines the quality of output, the best bet would be to provide fewer options, but higher standards.

Determine the service times according to when it would be best for the people.

Redefining "Success"

Think about the meaning of people's limited commitment. We know, for instance, that during the '90s we will begin to see the concept of the "church home" redefined. Already, people are choosing to have multiple church homes, in which they identify a handful of churches in the area that they feel comfortable with, and select from that handful on a given Sunday according to which one will best satisfy their felt needs that day. We also know that statistics related to church membership will continue their downward tumble.

This may require you to redefine "growth" or "membership" or "success" in ministry. The numbers game is changing, and so should our perceptions of what we are trying to achieve, and how we will measure the effect of our efforts.

Real and Relevant

Regardless of the definitions you use, no church will make gains unless it has integrity. This will be one of the first factors people will search for in the church—are these people "real," and can they be trusted, or is it simply a religious ritual, a social game they play? Like any other institution in America, the Church will be regarded with skepticism. We will be guilty, in the minds of millions of people, until proven innocent. Guilty of what? Irrelevance and unreliability.

Vision and Passion

How can you address this challenge? If you are seeking to minister to others, be sure you have God's vision for your ministry. Spend time in prayer, reading Scripture and studying the opportunities He has given you to reach others. Seek the advice of trusted leaders. God has a particular call to ministry for each of us who know Him and desire to represent Him to this world. If you want to radiate integrity, capture God's vision for your ministry, and pursue that vision with passion. Studies we have conducted of growing churches around the nation indisputably indicate that vision and passion are two central elements to attracting new people to the church and to faith in Christ.[1]

As we pursue our goals for ministry, be prepared to explain to people the difference between living according to a philosophy of life based on biblical principles, and the emptiness of having no guiding philosophy but making decisions haphazardly as we encounter opportunities and crises. Always, part of the function of those serving the Lord is to educate the world about God and His ways. The American people are more prone than ever to making life-changing decisions on the spur of the moment, without the benefit of a sense of the overall, long-term meaning of life and how to respond to conditions in ways consistent with that perspective. We ought to present a clear picture of how life can be more productive, less stressful, more meaningful and more enjoyable as a result of understanding how our faith integrates with our daily decisions and behavior.

When we strive to incorporate people into the life and ministry of the church, we also need to be extremely sensitive to the value of the time we are asking people to surrender. It is imperative that any programs or projects or services we engage in optimize the time of people—whether they are observers or participants. Because adults will guard their time so jealously, ministries that do not optimize that resource will lose people's interest and future involvement.

Gone are the days when a local church can take for granted that people will rise to the occasion when we call for volunteers to get involved. Gone are the days when we can expect a large portion of churched people to attend meetings or other church gatherings simply because the event is sponsored by the church. People will be selective in their participation. The church is in intense competition for people's time. The best way to assure that we will remain in the competition is to acknowledge the importance of people's time, and make the most of it when we are fortunate enough to receive it.

Note

1. George Barna, *Successful Churches: What They Have in Common* and *Church Growth: Practical Steps that Work* (Glendale, CA: Barna Research Group, 1990).

3 NEW WAYS OF SHARING WHAT WE KNOW

CHAPTER HIGHLIGHTS:

▶How fast an organization acquires data, and how efficiently it is used, will partly determine whether the organization survives.

▶We now have only 3 percent of the information that will be available to us by 2010. The key to surviving the approaching avalanche of information will be informed use, not the volume collected.

▶Expect significant new applications of existing technologies related to personal computers, satellites and telecommunications.

▶These new technologies must be embraced and utilized by the Church, and treated as a friend, not a foe. Church leaders must be technologically literate; staff may be added to handle the information flow. The very fact that the congregation is using the new technology sends an important signal to the surrounding community.

THE UNITED STATES HAS MADE THE TRANSITION FROM A MANUFACTUR-ing economy to one based upon the delivery of services. The fuel of this new economy has become information. More people than ever before spend their work days collecting, organizing, analyzing and reporting information. A major factor in the transformation has been the monumental breakthroughs in technology over the past two decades. The bold advances in technology and the resulting glut of information have forever changed the way we think, the way we perceive our world, the way we communicate, how we spend our time—in short, the way in which we live.

AMERICA, 1990

Boomers grew up hearing their parents marvel at the technological advances they witnessed during their lifetime: television, jet airplanes and space travel, automobiles, heart transplants, photocopiers, etc. The children of Boomers will grow up hearing *their* parents talk about life before personal computers, facsimile machines, cellular telephones, cable TV, microwave ovens and VCRs.

The effect of the intrusion of technology into our daily lives has been nothing short of phenomenal. While the learning curve is taking longer than many experts predicted, America has embraced the electronic world wholeheartedly. Our schedules are altered; the nature of the work we conduct is changed; the types of illnesses and aches we contract are different; and the ways in which we communicate with each other as a result of the machines and environment around us are new.

The electronic equipment introduced in the past decade or

so has altered the balance of world power. Today, information *is* power. It has redefined the critical factors for success in the marketplace. Speed of communications and information processing is essential for effective decision-making. Accessibility to these technologies is a minimum requirement to be competitive in the modern business environment. Executives who have served in the pre-computer and computer eras describe the difference in terms of "think time"; there is no longer time for reflection, since major and minor decisions alike require immediate access to relevant information and instant decisions in response.

Then and Now

Indeed, the change has been swift. The standard array of equipment in today's business office bears little resemblance to that which was common just ten years ago. At cutting edge companies in 1980, you were likely to find a multi-line telephone system with a switchboard operator. Secretaries typed memos and letters on electric typewriters. Materials that were urgently needed in distant locations were sent by overnight delivery. Presentations were prepared on acetate slides shown on an overhead projector, or perhaps via a multi-projector slide show (for the technologically advanced).

Today, you would be hard-pressed to find a major company which does not have personal computers at every work station; laser printers for both text and graphics output; a multiple-feature photocopier; and a facsimile machine for immediate transmission and reception of information. Increasing numbers of offices have replaced the switchboard operator with a tone-activated telephone system, with voice mail capabilities. Producing typeset-quality text and professional-quality graphics on an in-house computer is also common.

American industry, thanks to the lead of the Japanese, has made significant advances in the use of technology, too. High-speed printing presses produce thousands of tons of printed material every day. On-line information banks, containing entire libraries of publicly-available and proprietary data, are accessible 24-hours a day to companies networked into the system. Robots have been designed to perform many of the routine manufacturing functions that used to be done by assembly line workers.

Industrial studies indicate that people send and receive more information than ever, but spend less time actually communicating, in personal one-to-one conversation, with other people. When we do interact with each other, we have developed a new shorthand speech, frequently using numbers and statistics to make a point rather than using words and descriptions.

Even in our homes, the way we receive and send information has changed. Our color television sets provide more than two dozen channels of programming that operate 24 hours a day, received over cable lines. Most homes have VCRs, multiple radios (an average of five), audiocassette decks, and several telephones throughout the home. Millions of households have answering machines, to screen calls or to record messages during the owner's absence. Long-distance telephone calls are likely to be transmitted across fiber optic lines for greater clarity and efficiency.

The majority of our public schools (85 percent) use computers to teach students. (In fact, computer literacy may become one of the issues related to educational quality in the '90s.) Television is even becoming a part of the formal in-school experience, with two major media corporations (Whittle and Turner Broadcasting) providing daily news programming to classrooms. Videocassettes have become a standard educational tool.

You're in Someone's Data Bank

New data base management systems have further enabled marketers to target their messages to very finite audiences. Organizations such as Donnelly Marketing can now make available detailed information about more than 85 million of our 92 million households. Based upon combined data bases and statistical modeling techniques, these systems can describe, with great accuracy, your television viewing patterns, radio listening

---

Although we have an incredible amount of information available already, the volume is just 3 percent of what we will have at our fingertips in 2010!

---

habits, magazine and newspaper reading preferences, product purchasing by brand, household demographics and key attitudes and values. This information can then be incorporated into multi-million piece mailings, sent only to households that represent the highest potential for sales of any given product.

In fact, although communications have become less personal in their delivery form, we are receiving more information all the time. Today, we are exposed to an estimated 1500 commercial messages per day. There are over 10,000 magazines published in America, complementing the 6,000 radio stations and 400 television stations. Your mailbox is stuffed with mail from people and companies you have never heard of, but who seem to know quite a bit about your spending habits and interests. In fact, last year there were more than 100 different catalogs per household printed in the U.S. The average home received more than 1,000 pieces of unsolicited mail during the year.

One teacher, in assessing the impact of these many changes

in the information landscape, suggested that we have become "the most overstimulated society in history." And it's only just begun....

AMERICA, 2000

Futurist Roger Selbert has stated that although we have an incredible amount of information available already, the volume is just 3 percent of what we will have at our fingertips in 2010! Thus, we will experience yet another information explosion during the coming quarter century. The key to benefiting from that explosion, however, will not be in hording the overwhelming volume of new data, but in being able to quickly identify the most useful information and then applying that information to daily activities for greater impact.

The '80s were a time for many technological breakthroughs, a time of converting theory into practical invention. The '90s will be a time of developing practical applications, making the initial breakthroughs even more significant. Applications will come in the form of new uses of the computer, our satellite inventory and the telecommunications infrastructure.

Computers at Work

Several decades ago, a few forward thinkers predicted that computers would gain widespread usage and create the paperless office. Well, they were partially right. Computers are here to stay, and will become more powerful, faster and smaller in the next decade. But they create *more* paper, rather than less. In fact, they will create new uses for paper in the future. Consider, for example, that by the mid-'90s, television sets will be sold with hook-ups for a computer printer, allowing viewers to print coupons for advertised products in which they are interested. Some households will replace the morning newspaper with an electronic version, which they can read on the monitor of their home computer. This videotex communication process can be printed out as necessary.

Computers are currently in 1 out of every 4 American homes. As household applications become more prevalent and simpler to run, and as younger adults who have been weaned on computers in school come of age, this proportion will rise to nearly one out of every two homes by the year 2000. Our social institutions will rise to the occasion, too. Libraries will provide more checked out materials on diskette. Homework assignments will be routinely turned in on diskettes, and checked by the master computer at school. Certain government communications will be distributed through diskettes. Encyclopedia sets will be replaced by CD-ROM disk systems, in which the entire encyclopedia is included on a single plastic disk, with rapid access. This system is already in use, but it will not be available at widely affordable prices for another five years or so.

Smart Cards—and Highways, Too

Optical scanners will make computers even more versatile. Currently, there are perhaps 100,000 scanners being used for desktop computer operations. By 2000, thanks to advances in software applications and the quality of the scanning technology, that number will exceed 4 million.

Scanners will also enhance our life in the marketplace. By mid-decade, scanners in grocery stores will enable us to have self-checkout lines. Once the total cost of our groceries has been determined, we will be able to pay using our "smart card," which will be a financial account activator, a combination of the ATM card and a credit card. Carrying money with us will not be necessary, although cash will still be an acceptable form of legal tender.

With a space station planted outside the earth's orbit, and

satellites surrounding the globe, we will have tremendous capabilities to use information transmitted via satellites. Most cars, for instance, will have computers managing the entire functioning of the engine systems. By 2000, auto manufacturers will offer car buyers the option of a satellite navigation system, in which the video display screen mounted in your dashboard will show you the optimal route to take, given your destination. Using up-to-the-second data on traffic jams, street conditions and the weather, the navigation system will even indicate to you when you should be turning.[1] (By the middle of the next century, it is likely that our roadways will have special devices implanted which will enable computer-programmed autos to actually drive the vehicle to our destination.)

Phone Mail, Phone Malls

We will still be communicating by telephone, but in profoundly different ways. Your telephone number will be 10 digits long, due to the fact that in the mid-'90s we will run out of telephone numbers using the current seven digit system. Although fiber optics networks will be more prevalent, the cost and time required for replacing the existing copper cable system will cause the introduction of an interim technology: ISDN (integrated services digital network). This technology will allow you to transmit combination of audio, text, video and data over telephone lines, providing enhanced capabilities for transmitting and retrieving complex sets of information and data.

The telephone will also be used with cable TV and computers to provide shoppers with an electronic "mall." Using interactive technology, you will be able to shop at the mall without leaving your living room. Simply turn on the TV, and using your telephone and a computer keyboard, select from menu-driven directories which stores in the mall you'd like to visit. Your screen will show you the entrance of the store; select your desired department, and you will see the entrance of that department. Using additional prompts, you will be able to view merchandise within the department, read and hear descriptions of the items, and place an order. The purchase will be charged to your account, and delivered the next morning.

Nor will the telephone remain attached to the wall. With fewer than 250,000 cellular car phones in service in 1990,

---

"Smart houses" will automatically control all indoor functions—turning on the lights, changing the room temperature according to who is in the room, activating the television set and the security system upon command.

---

expect car phones to be more common by 2000. Experts expect more than 10 million cars to be wired by 1995. In addition, millions of other people will invest in the "pocket phone," a portable telephone which can be folded into the size of a man's wallet, and carried around in one's pocket. Using satellite technology, these instruments will be common in 2000, enabling us to be accessible no matter where we travel.

The fax machine will experience increased market penetration during the '90s. Now residing in 5 million businesses and homes, the penetration will expand to six times this figure by the turn of the century. Expect to find advances in the quality of transmissions, color faxing and larger-sized fax transmissions.

Be warned: you may find that your car becomes your office, too. Automobiles are now available which provide all the needs of an office—a battery-driven computer and printer, a fax machine that works on batteries and transmits via satellite connection and a laptop copier, run on batteries. Naturally, a cellular telephone is part of the operation. Although few of these offices-on-wheels are presently cruising the streets, they will gain widespread acceptance in the years ahead, and will enable many traveling sales representatives to conduct their business more efficiently.

Two-way video teleconferencing is currently used by more than 1,000 corporations nationwide. Organizations such as Sears, J.C. Penney, Boeing, Apple Computers and even the Manhattan District Attorney's office use satellite-transmitted interactive video technology for regular meetings, connecting different branch offices for updating and decision-making. On the home front, although primitive versions of the picture-phone will be available, the costs will make these devices prohibitive.

Advances in artificial intelligence software will permit voice recognition systems to proliferate. Computers will take dictation. Telephone systems will connect your call without your having to dial a number. Once your call is answered, a voice recognition answering system will transfer your call to the party desired. Corporate and home security systems will be based on "voiceprints"—a sample of your speech, which will act as your secret pass for entry into your home, or security-conscious offices.

Artificial Intelligence (AI), however, will go far beyond mere voice recognition. Advanced AI will permit many middle management positions to be eliminated, providing the types of data analysis and reporting now performed by mid-level staff people. In addition, robots will be developed which will perform basic, routine functions both in business (burger flipping, hospital orderly functions) and at home. However, before we can expect to see the types of mobile robots that are featured in science fiction movies, we will have to radically redesign our homes, offices and furniture to accommodate their mobility limitations.

Smart World

What else could they possibily devise in the next ten years? Plenty. You will be able to purchase a "smart house"—one that automatically controls all indoor functions, from turning on the lights as you enter a room, to changing the room temperature according to who is in the room, to voice activating the television set or stereo, to activating the security system upon command. You might also purchase a "smart TV"—which will record programs you miss, and automatically show you the programs you are most likely to watch when you are home. Preprogrammed to understand your viewing tastes, this TV will be tied into a central database of upcoming programs to provide for your viewing interests, regardless of your schedule limitations.

Your hot air clothes dryer will be replaced by a microwave clothes dryer. Genetic advances will provide us with the gardener's dream—a self-weeding lawn—by 1993. Today's building materials will be replaced by new super-strong materials such as glass, ceramics and plastics with the strength of metal. Highways will be paved with synthetic materials for greater durability and technological innovations.

Certainly, the days ahead will bring new technological toy after new technological toy. The real benefits, however, will be in the impact on our quality of life. We will have faster and deeper access to information and knowledge. We will save time, and be freed from the tyranny of on-location business.

Realize, too, that these are only the advances that can be readily predicted today. Potential developments in fusion energy, photonics and optical microprocessors will catapult us faster and farther along than most of us care to dream about.

Will Americans feverishly accept these new devices and the resulting changes in life-style? More likely than not, people will grudgingly accept these advances, much like a sick person swallows a foul-tasting medicine—confident that the prescription will help, but not cheerful about the discomfort caused by the remedy. As we age, we will also retard the rate of acceptance of new gadgets and equipment. However, since many of the new products will enable us to enjoy more productive leisure time, or to upgrade our quality of life, acceptance will be a matter of time more than a matter of principle.

✝ CHALLENGES AND OPPORTUNITIES FOR THE CHURCH

While many of the televangelist ministries have been innovators in communications technology (Pat Robertson and Oral Roberts have used cutting edge technology for years), the local church has rarely been in the forefront of the movement. In fact, research has suggested that churches are among the last organizations to accept new technology. In 1990, only 50 percent of our churches even own a computer. Most of those use the machines for simple tasks, such as word processing and basic accounting.

In a society driven by speed and information, it is imperative to invest in useful technology. Few would expect the church to be a showcase for the newest innovations. However, as time goes on, more and more people will expect the Church to at least be in the game technologically. Owning equipment such as personal computers, laser printers and fax machines will not only expedite the flow of information and the timely completion of business, but will also send a signal to the community that the Church is relevant and informed about what's really going on in society. It will be increasingly difficult to convince the unchurched, and those who are questioning Christianity, that our faith is pertinent to the 21st century if the tools of our trade are from the last century.

Technology Invades the Church

*Percentage of local churches equipped
with recent communications technology:*

83%

49%

21%

| 1985 | 1990 | 2000 |

Computers

38%

0%   **4%**

| 1985 | 1990 | 2000 |

Fax Machines

89%

68%

32%

| 1985 | 1990 | 2000 |

VCR

Source: Barna Research Group

Clergy must become technologically literate in the days ahead. This simply means being able to use a computer or a fax machine. Understanding the value and applications of desktop publishing and desktop video. Able to operate a video camera. Even if our seminaries do not begin to prepare and train ministers for such responsibilities, the clergy (and lay leaders, as applicable) must develop skills that will permit them to use technology for the benefit of ministry.

The effective church of 2000 will be technologically savvy. People will expect services to incorporate video. Communications ought to look sharp, produced through desktop publishing facilities. Bulletins might be faxed to members in advance of Sunday. Members might be able to tie into the church's schedule and Scripture data base through modems in their home computer. Growing churches will position themselves as spiritual resource centers, providing their people with easily accessible and pertinent data for spiritual growth.

As the pace of information flow accelerates, pastors (in particular) must realize that accessibility to decision-makers and key individuals is critical. Remaining inaccessible to the congregation will not work. Either the pastor or recognized designees must be available to handle people's inquiries at the time the call or transmission occurs. Time, more than ever, will be of the essence. Your competitors—that is, government officials, manufacturers, sales rep—will take steps to become more accessible. The church must be prepared to do the same, or gain the image of aloofness.

Also expect to feel the need for a new staff position: information management specialist. Most corporations already have such people. They track trends, develop the internal data base, catalog information and report new insights emerging from the influx of new information received. As churches evaluate budgets, attendance and participation figures, reactions to new programs, community population statistics and the like, someone must be responsible for this data, and how it is handled. Consider the benefit of developing an information management system now, one which will allow expansion as your needs and environment change.

Note
1. Malcolm Abrams and Harriet Bernstein, *Future Stuff* (New York: Penguin Books, 1989), p. 272.

4 THE SHAPE OF OUR FAMILIES AND FRIENDS

CHAPTER HIGHLIGHTS:

▶New forms of family: single-parent families, blended families, cohabitating adults and street gangs.

▶Divorce and multiple marriages will be the norm...as will be predictable periods of divorce and remarriage in people's lives.

▶Loneliness will become even more widespread, as our usual sources for developing friendships are displaced, and our skills at creating and maintaining friendships erode.

▶Great opportunities for the church to become:

–A center for the development of friendships

–A source of insight into and practical skills in personal relationships and communication

–A place to celebrate successful, working examples of marriages and family, and solving tough issues in family relationships. ▶▶▶▶▶

THE TRADITIONAL FAMILY IS DEAD." "WE HAVE BECOME A NATION OF friendless adults." "Marriage is an outdated institution." Read any magazine or newspaper article about the days ahead, and you are likely to encounter such dramatic statements. While some journalists have exaggerated the state of affairs regarding the family and friendships in America, they have captured the spirit of the changes likely in the next decade.

 AMERICA, 1990

The reported disintegration of the family is not an accurate portrayal of the American condition. What *has* happened is that the *traditional* family unit—the working father and a mother who stays home to care for the two children—has been replaced by a different type of household. In 1960, this stereo-typical family type represented 60 percent of all households; today, it reflects just 7 percent of our households.

The average American family in 1990 consists of a married couple with one child, in which both parents are employed. At least one of the parents is likely to have been divorced, or will be divorced. Parents are having fewer children and having them later in life. Increasing proportions of households are "blended families"—homes in which the children from two or more marriages are combined as a result of remarriages. There is also a growing trend toward partners having children without being married. In 1990, about one out of every fifteen children will be born out of wedlock.

When Practice Doesn't Make Perfect

Although we think of the "Woodstock generation" as the era in which couples were most likely to live together outside of mar-

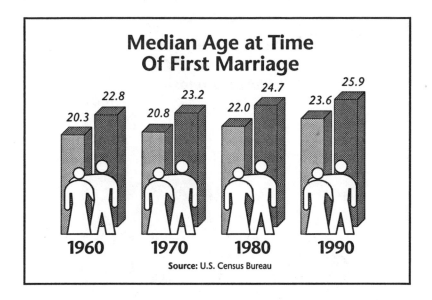

Median Age at Time Of First Marriage

20.3 22.8 20.8 23.2 22.0 24.7 23.6 25.9

1960 1970 1980 1990

Source: U.S. Census Bureau

riage, cohabitation is more prevalent today than ever. Half of all adults under the age of 30 will live with someone before they get married. Sixty percent of recently-married adults indicate that they lived with their new spouse before getting married. While unmarried, cohabitating adults constitute a small percentage of all households, it is the fastest growing household arrangement. The proportion of households headed by unmarried people living together has quadrupled since 1970.

This "trial household" approach has not done much for marital stability, however. Census Bureau statistics suggest that people who cohabitate before marriage are even more likely than others to get divorced. Apparently, practice does *not* make perfect when it comes to marriage. Among people who have been divorced and remarried, 60 percent of all second marriages end in divorce.[1]

Presently, one out of four households consists of a single parent with one or more children. The trends indicate that of all the children born in 1990, six out of ten will live in a single-

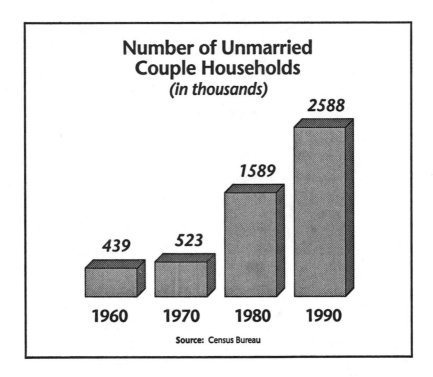

Number of Unmarried Couple Households
(in thousands)

2588

1589

439   523

1960   1970   1980   1990

Source: Census Bureau

parent household for some period of time before they reach the age of 18.

Perhaps these statistics are less surprising when we consider the attitudes of adults toward marriage, sex and family. Two-thirds of all adults under 50 had pre-marital sex, and just 8 percent regret having done so.[2] The perceived value of a stable marriage has also tumbled, as 70 percent of all adults in this country believe that if a couple with young children cannot get along, they should not stay together simply for the sake of the children.[3]

Despite our seemingly difficult experiences with, and negative attitudes toward, marriage and family, survey after survey report that people's greatest source of happiness in life is family. This has consistently been true over the last 30 years.

However, there is a new twist to the information. In addition to describing the family as their source of greatest pleasure and satisfaction, adults explain that this delight is a result of being able to pursue their own interests and needs. In other words, adults want to have their cake and eat it, too. As long as the responsibilities of family life do not hinder us from pursuing our varied interests, then family may be a great source of joy. A little publicized fact is that several surveys have also found that the greatest source of frustration and disappointment in people's lives is dealing with family problems.

New Ideals for Women

Perhaps nothing clarifies this condition better than the development of the typical American female. The ideals of women in the '50s and '60s revolved around motherhood and home. In the '70s and '80s, increasingly the dream focused upon being accepted as an equal in the labor force, and having fewer family-related constraints. Today, the average American woman believes that it is her right to be a mother and a career woman, as well as to have a marriage relationship that is void of conflict and tension. If her marriage contains such pressures, she feels free to leave the relationship, with child in tow.

The increasing prevalence of divorce and working women has turned child care into a major growth industry. Here again we can see the shift in people's priorities. In the '60s and earlier, the dominant goal in life for most mothers was to raise healthy, happy, well-adjusted children. Today, the goal of most parents (men and women) is to be personally fulfilled in all walks of life. The fact that 81 percent of working mothers, and 92 percent of all working mothers with preschool children describe available child care options as below their expectations has not hindered them from making use of those services.[4] The average working parent spends about $2,500 a year on child care assistance.

The family unit itself behaves quite differently today than in the past, too. We spend less time together than previously. Meals are less likely to be eaten at home as a shared family experience. Vacations are shorter and less likely to include all members of the household. The average home now has multiple television sets, enabling children and adults to watch different programming in separate rooms. Our youths are more mobile and self-sufficient than ever.

Older Youth—Sooner
Indeed, our young people are taking on adult behaviors and responsibilities at younger ages than ever. On average, young people experience sexual intercourse for the first time at age 16. One-third of all teenagers who have reached driving age *own* a car. Teenagers, as a group, receive $50-55 billion in income each year. They are responsible for substantial discretionary spending, in addition to household buying duties. Surveys indicate that about three out of four teens are responsible for some of their household's regular shopping.[5]

At the same time, children who live with their parents report that they spend less than 30 minutes *per week* in meaningful conversation with their mothers, and less than 15 minutes per week in meaningful conversation with their father.

Friendships—Desire and Disappointment
One outcome of the changing nature of family relationships is that we are seeking emotional gratification from sources outside of the home. Friendships are earnestly desired by more and more Americans, as the pressures within the home drive us to seek consolation, appreciation, encouragement, and understanding elsewhere.

Unfortunately, America is a nation in which the yearning

for strong friendships far exceeds their existence. The majority of Americans feel that they do not have enough close friends. Among the reasons why we struggle with building and maintaining significant relationships are the high level of transience, which tears us away from those whom we have become friendly with; our inability, as a nation, to effectively communicate with each other; the fragmentation of our schedules,

---

By 2000, Americans will generally believe that a life spent with the same partner is both unusual and unnecessary.

---

which makes sharing time together difficult; and the shifts in attitudes that make us less willing to make commitments to long-term relationships.

 AMERICA, 2000

Marriage will certainly not be dismissed as a viable life-style within the next decade. The desire for companionship and a fulfilling family life will cause people to continue marrying...over and over again. While Americans may be prone to discarding traditional conventions, marriage will not be one which is dissolved.

The biggest change will come not in the disinterest in marriage, but in the acceptance of divorce as a part of the marriage process. By 2000, Americans will generally believe that a life spent with the same partner is both unusual and unnecessary. We will continue our current moral transition by accepting sexual relationships with one person at a time—"serial monogamy"—to be the civilized and moral way to behave. But we will not consider it at all unusual to be married two or three times during the course of life.

There will be a dramatic rise in the number of multi-generational households. Having three or four generations living under the same roof will be more and more common.

People will begin to consciously acknowledge that they are likely to have several spouses over the course of their lifetime, and will choose partners who will best satisfy their needs during the different periods of their life. Instead of thinking about marriage as a lifelong commitment, we will perceive it to be a temporary union.

Remarriage will occur most commonly during the transition from one life stage to another: from youth to young adulthood and family-rearing; from the emptying of the nest to entry into middle age and career achievement; from career wind-down to retirement and leisure; and from active leisure to aged maturity and the need for companionship and physical care. Age will become less of a factor in selecting a partner than the ability of a prospective partner to satiate our physical and emotional needs at that stage of our life.

Our attitudes about marital relationships will not return to the traditional models. As majorities of our young adults emerge from the hardship of growing up in blended families, they will look to their own marriages as a mark of independence. Marriage will be viewed as their chance to receive the emotional gratification that was absent in their lives as they were growing up. Rather than changing the prevailing attitudes and behaviors that created such turmoil in their maturing years by establishing a more traditional marriage relationship, they will seek to get what they feel is rightfully theirs, regardless of the implications for their own children. Such will be the mindset of America in 2000: the "look out for number one" mentality will persist, albeit with some smoothed edges that make the philosophy appear to be morally and socially acceptable.

Ganging Up as "Family"

Apart from changes in marriage and household structure, America is already experiencing what will become one of the prevalent new family forms: street gangs. For thousands of adolescents, gangs are a response to the dissolution of the traditional family. Membership in a gang provides the only place where some young people find they can get a fair hearing and response to the daily pressures, doubts and struggles they face.

The saving grace for our communities is that there will be fewer young adults available to join gangs in 2000. However, even with reduced numbers of gang members, police squads will frequently be incapable of stopping gang violence and crime. In Los Angeles, for instance, gang members outnumber police by ten to one. Initially found only in our largest cities, gangs will be a nationwide reality by 2000. In a sense, they will be the Mafia of the early 21st century, trafficking in drugs, pornography and information. The need for social acceptance will strengthen the presence of gangs drawn along racial and ethnic lines. Gangs will represent most of the major ethnic and racial groups found in our cities.

Lonely in the Crowd

Because the factors that have led to rampant loneliness and emotional emptiness show no signs of dissipating, it is unlikely that Americans will feel any less lonely 10 years from now than they do today. Many of the tangible results of our loneliness —alcoholism, drug abuse, physical abuse, suicide, depression, sexual promiscuity—are not likely to subside to any noticeable degree. Certain manifestations—such as premarital sex—are likely to increase, as our attitudes about relationships become increasingly liberal and permissive. Interestingly, we will become less judgmental of others in these areas, simply because we do not want to be judged by others.

Child care will continue as a boom industry for the first half of the decade, until the demographic curves related to the presence of young children begin to descend. Elder care will blossom as a major industry during the '90s. The cost of such intensive care, however, will also bring about a dramatic rise in the number of multi-generational households. Having three or four generations living under the same roof will be more and more common. This will likely lead to higher tension in homes, due to spatial limitations, clashes between the different values of the generations represented and the increased likelihood of elderly abuse.

Homes in the '90s

Housing will also undergo some interesting transformations. Because of the frequency with which we will move to new locations, change partners and blend offspring, and because of the likelihood of economic upheavals in the early '90s, we will rent and lease homes more, instead of buying. This will reduce the property settlement battles after divorce, and expedite the forming of new living arrangements.

We will also witness the introduction of a common European form of housing, called cohousing. Neighborhoods are designed by the residents, providing clusters of private dwellings with shared community facilities (laundry, day care, dining areas, guest rooms, recreation facilities). People's private

---

We must help people rediscover the meaning of our marriage vows, and the possibilities inherent in a long-term commitment to each other.

---

living space is reduced, but remains adaptable to the person's changes in life-style and family design. In Denmark and other places in Europe, this approach has been found to encourage greater social interaction and to reduce stresses related to housing needs and maintenance.[6]

Friendships will be ever harder to come by. Not only will we struggle with our current limitations—transience, poor communication skills, fragmented schedules and unwillingness to make long-term commitments to others—we will have new obstacles to add to the mix. The major new barrier will be the reduced opportunities to meet people of like backgrounds and goals. With employment becoming more decentralized, due to technological advances leading to more people working from their homes, we will lack the face-to-face encounters with people at work. The '90s will also be a time when women assume greater roles of responsibility in the workplace, thus increasing their commitment to career rather than to personal interactions.

✝ CHALLENGES AND OPPORTUNITIES FOR THE CHURCH

Some social scientists have argued that the strength of America has been its family stability. During times of great change, uncertainty and experimentation, we have survived because of our ability to cling to the relationships at home which brought us a semblance of peace, happiness and assurance.

The coming century will be a time of great change, uncertainty and experimentation. It will also be a time in which the traditional comfort zone provided by the family will no longer be present.

Where will the Church be during this time of searching? Will we be continuing to do our religious thing on Sunday mornings, oblivious to the undercurrent of instability, or will we be active in supporting a more cohesive, traditional form of the family, as portrayed in the Bible? Unless the Christian Church provides creative, intelligent and forceful arguments on behalf of the family structure designed by God for mankind, it is unlikely that the gap will be filled by any other institution.

And what about discussions regarding premarital sex? The current plateauing of such unions is largely in reaction to the spread of AIDS. Suppose scientists discover a cure or preventive measure for AIDS. Will the Church be silent, or will it provide a serious response to people's penchant for exploring sexual relations with a variety of partners? The tragedy of today's warnings about sexual promiscuity is that they exclude morality as a basis for determining proper behavior. Certainly, the Church can help to fill the moral void by offering sound arguments for sexual behavior, using Christian moral standards as a reasonable point of consideration.

Defining the Church's Role

As we move away from the traditional understanding of parenting roles and responsibilities, it is likely that the Church will be the last major institution to champion the conventional family model. During the '90s, we must define the Church's role as one of educating people about the benefits of permanent monogamy and of intense family relationships. If we truly believe that God has ordained marriage and family according to the traditional understanding of those unions, then we must mount a new and aggressive campaign to shift the course of Americans' attitudes and behavior. Part of that campaign must be to celebrate those families and marriages which are making it. Events geared to encouraging those, and other families will be integral to supporting families through the rocky periods of most marriages.

Part of our response to the pressures on today's family unit may be to provide more extensive and valued premarital counseling to individuals seeking to become husband and wife. In addition to the typical emphasis upon honesty and communication, we must help people rediscover the meaning of our vows, and the possibilities inherent in a long-term commitment to each other.

The Church ought to consider a consistent celebration of marriage, too—not simply wailing about the demise of relationships, but publicly treasuring the successful marriages in our midst. Americans learn best by behavioral modeling. Knowing that marriage does work, and being sensitive to the volume of marriages that work successfully, would enhance our ability to persuade people to rethink the place of divorce and "serial monogamy" in their lives.

While we uphold the importance of marriage, we cannot reject people who are divorced, or who struggle with the need to extricate themselves from a destructive marriage. Post-marital counseling must be available to help people through the rocky times. Ways to reach out to, and accept, single parents must be found. Churches must offer counseling programs, support groups, recreational opportunities for the children of single parents and other services that help these adults to be the kind of parents they want to be.

Taking Gangs Seriously

In addition to focusing on the relationship between the marriage partners, and the needs of single parents, churches also have a responsibility to children. In several cities around the U.S., churches have taken a leading role in addressing the street gang situation. They are providing evening activities as an alternative to violence and crime; discussion forums to air their problems and concerns in an atmosphere of love and acceptance; and negotiating services to ease tensions between existing gangs.

More churches must acknowledge the reality of gangs, and the pressures of growing up in America today. We must provide relevant alternatives to gangs and other non-family life-styles. Youth ministry, often seen as a form of sophisticated baby-sitting, must be viewed instead as a critical part of the education and socialization of our youth.

Layered into all of the educational processes outlined above must be an intensified effort at helping people to communicate. Unfortunately, the Church itself has not been effective at this process. We tend to provide information, but we are less skilled at the other vital part of the communication process —listening. Yet, we have to help people incorporate better total communication skills into their lives if we are to have an opportunity to help them develop any meaningful relationships. Since the nation's schools devote little time to honing these skills, the Church must help to plug the gap.

Many churches already offer child care programs and facilities for the community. This has proved to be a vital ministry for those churches that view this as more than simply a money-making opportunity or baby-sitting service. By instilling positive values in young children, teaching them early on the value and skills of effective communication and causing them to feel comfortable being at a church, long-term benefits will be realized. Similarly, the impact of the Church's relevance and presence in the life of many nonchurched adults has also proved to be a positive step in their renewed interest in Christianity.

Looking Out for the Lonely

Perhaps as much as anything else, though, the Church is better poised than any other institution in America to respond to the rampant loneliness of the American people. In addition to bringing people together on a regular basis, the Church has the potential to create lasting bonds between people who can share common interests and common goals. As more and more adults search for opportunities to meet other people, one of the greatest selling points of the Church in the coming decade will be the ability to meet other people from the community. Systems, policies, programs and procedures which capitalize upon this felt need will enable churches to grow in numbers, in depth of ministry and in the ability to celebrate the love of Christ poured out through His people.

Notes
1. Barbara Kantrowitz and Pat Wingert, "Step by Step," *Newsweek* (Special issue, Winger/Spring, 1990), pp. 24-34.
2. David Sheff, "Portrait of a Generation," *Rolling Stone*, May 5, 1988, pp. 46-65.
3. Statistics from a Gallup Poll, reported in *Newsweek*, op. cit., p. 18.
4. Data supplied by Louis Harris Organization, New York, NY.
5. Lawrence Graham and Lawrence Hamdan, *Youth Trends* (New York: St. Martin's Press, 1987), p. 3.
6. *The Futurist*, September/October 1989, pp. 23-32.

5 THE GOOD TIMES: AMERICA AT PLAY

CHAPTER HIGHLIGHTS:

▶*Leisure*—one of Americans' most treasured resources—has gained prominence in our life-styles and become more diverse and fragmented.
▶During the '90s, leisure will be even more important both as refreshment and as a source of meaning in life.
▶Increased time for leisure will alter how we approach our free time. Look for changes in volunteerism, community events and our involvement with the mass media.
▶To remain relevant and competitive, churches must adapt extra-curricular programs to focus on entertainment, value-added events, current media centers and the intelligent use and motivation of volunteers. ▶▶▶▶▶

Y̲OU CAN TAKE AWAY OUR JOBS, YOU CAN CLOSE DOWN THE CHURCHES, you may tear apart our families—but don't ever try to restrict the play time of Americans. Many adults devote greater concentration and effort to making the most of their leisure hours than they commit to their productivity on the job. Our philosophy and practices related to leisure activity explain much about American perspectives on life, happiness and values.

 AMERICA, 1990

Rolling Stone magazine conducted a massive national study in 1988 to explore people's attitudes about the past and the future. Among the findings: If adults had one extra hour a day, they would be most likely to spend it on leisure or recreational activities.[1]

Another study shows that the average adult spends less time working now than was the case 25 years ago. The number of hours spent on the job has decreased from 49 hours per week to 42 among men; and from 39 hours per week to 31 among women. What has filled the gap? Housework? Educational pursuits? Involvement with our children? Try recreational activities, which have jumped by more than 10 percent in the amount of time given to them.[2]

We are not a society that simply enjoys its time off. We are *driven* by our leisure appetites. It is increasingly common to hear of people turning down job offers because the hours or other responsibilities would interfere with their hobbies, fitness regimens and other free time activities. Even our spending habits show that playing has become a major priority. The average household spends more money on entertainment than it does on clothing, health care, furniture or gasoline.[3]

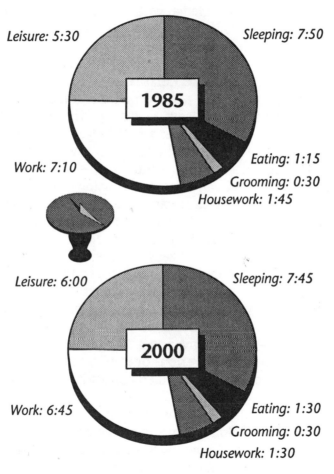

24 Hours a Day:
How We Spend Our Time

Leisure: 5:30   Sleeping: 7:50

1985

Work: 7:10   Eating: 1:15
Grooming: 0:30
Housework: 1:45

Leisure: 6:00   Sleeping: 7:45

2000

Work: 6:45   Eating: 1:30
Grooming: 0:30
Housework: 1:30

Source: data and projections based upon
Americans' Use of Time Project, Survey
Research Center, University of Maryland

Much of our entertainment intake is through the mass media. Media research studies indicate that consumers spend about five hours a day absorbing media: about three hours watching television, an hour with radio and another hour reading newspapers and magazines. Clearly, Americans are heavily exposed to the media, with television responsible for the bulk of that exposure.

The Shift to Productive Leisure

As leisure endeavors have taken on a more important role in our lives, we have also begun to reshape the nature of our leisure pursuits. Leisure activities are no longer simply "feet up" times in which we pop on the TV and passively observe moving images for hours at a time. More and more, leisure simply refers to non-occupational activities. We are slowly moving away from devotion to mindless, time-filler forms of relaxation toward an engagement with active, purposeful activities.

This shift can be seen by observing the differences between Baby Boomers and senior citizens. Boomers are more likely to engage in productive leisure (e.g., exercise and physical fitness, cultural events). They are attracted to free time activities that have a tangible, valued outcome: learning, health, emotional investment, cultural enhancement. Seniors, in contrast, prefer playful leisure—travel, cards and other games based on luck, events in which nothing serious or intellectually taxing takes place (dances, contests) and similarly pleasing but non-progressive efforts.

It may well be that this growing focus on productive leisure helps to explain the discrepancy between how much time we spend on the job, and how much time we *think* we spend on the job. While the research reported earlier shows that we are actually committing fewer hours to work, Americans *believe* that they are now putting in more time than in prior years. It is conceivable that because we have blurred some of the distinctions between work and play, we feel more work-involved than we really are.

With society becoming increasingly complex, demanding and stress-inducing, Americans are relying upon their free time to make life worthwhile. Toward that end, we are striving to have a variety of experiences, each delivering top quality, and remaining conveniently accessible.

To satisfy our hunger for multiple experiences, we allocate shorter blocks of time for any single leisure activity. As a nation we believe that the more different experiences we have, the more likely we will be to find fulfillment.

Leisure in Bits

Today, to satisfy our hunger for multiple experiences, we allocate shorter blocks of time for any single leisure activity. As a nation, we believe that the more different experiences we have, the more likely we will be to find fulfillment. This is partially an outgrowth of the Boomers' belief in experimentation. Just as they experimented with drugs in the '60s, they are now seeking a broader base of adventures in all phases of their lives.

In part, breaking our leisure time into smaller chunks is a response to our hectic schedules. Because we want to experience so much, but have limited time in which to do so, our best option is to give up time-consuming endeavors. Few people are willing to consistently devote two- or three-hour periods to a single activity. And who could possibly coordinate the tight, fragmented schedules of the eight or more people it takes to play most team sports? As a result, even our choice of activities has shifted significantly. Lengthy, people-intensive games like baseball and football are less attractive. In their place, we see individualized sports such as tennis, jogging, racquetball and swimming gaining in popularity.

Physical fitness activities apart from individual or team sports have boomed. Once deemed a mere fad, the combination of dieting and regular exercise has become a multiple-billion dollar industry in the U.S. Not only are more people becoming active in fitness activities, but the age range at which such efforts are common is expanding. More elderly people than ever before are including exercise walking, jogging, bicycling, aerobics, golf and swimming as part of their daily regimen.

One of the most encouraging aspects of the fitness craze has been a related shift away from the consumption of hard liquor to beer and wine. The per capita consumption of liquor has dropped consistently for the past several years, while beer, in particular, has benefited from this change in habit. At the same time, we have also seen a dip in the proportion of adults and teenagers involved in the regular use of drugs.

Leisure in Bytes
Our desire to jam as many experiences into as short a period as possible is even impacting the way we schedule vacations. Rather than taking the traditional two-week vacation at a single time, the trend is toward shorter vacations—two and three days plus a weekend.

Another major transition in how we spend our free time is making our homes the hub of leisure pursuit. Technology has brought new forms of entertainment into the home, through the likes of VCRs, pay-per-view cable channels, sophisticated

Social Activism:
The Causes that Stimulate Action

Major Causes of the '60s	**Major Causes of the '90s**
Racial equality	Environmental protection
Women's liberation	Substance abuse
Industrial pollution	Neighborhood crime/ street gangs
Rent control	
World peace	Global economic stability
Police brutality	Nuclear disarmament
Urban development	Foreign investment in America
Cold war	
Government regulation	Corporate ethics
Poverty	Abortion
International imperialism	Garbage
Cancer	Health care costs
Birth control	AIDS
Sexual morality	Poverty
	Illiteracy
	Public transportation
	Information management
	Water conservation
	Artificial intelligence
	Medical ethics
	Elder care

in-home exercise equipment and computer games. With delivery services bringing pizza, Chinese food, and even videos to our doorstep upon request, more and more families come home at the end of the work day, determine their pleasure for the night, and allow those forms of entertainment to unravel in the comfort of their home.

AMERICA, 2000

During the coming decade, the value of leisure time will heighten because people will find less and less fulfillment from their jobs, their marriages and their existing social networks.

Boomers, always a group who recognized the value of play, will increasingly turn to leisure pursuits to find meaning in life. For millions of Boomers, the rise to positions of responsibility and influence within the corporate world will seem like a hollow victory. Senior citizens, who will be more numerous than at any prior time in our history, will concentrate on making the most of their accumulation of both wealth and free time.

Perhaps more importantly, the changes in the nature of the labor force—an expanded segment of older adults with highly technical or executive responsibilities, and a growing base of low-skilled workers earning minimal wages—will lead to a population that depends upon leisure activity for fulfillment and satisfaction in life.

Because of our dedication to satisfying leisure experiences, and because of transitions within the workplace, we can expect the amount of free time we can control to expand over current levels of nonwork time by 10-15 percent.

Free and Together
The ways in which we spend that time will differ in some ways from how we use free time today. One of our preoccupations

will be involvement in activities that enable us to build a greater number of solid personal relationships. Although people will not be willing to join organizations or institutions as formal members, they will affiliate with organizations that facilitate meaningful interaction with other people of like interests and backgrounds.

Among the activities that will bring people together for relational purposes will be activist movements and organizations seeking to develop grassroots response to various social ills. People will continue to devote large amounts of time to volunteer activities, although they will be more selective about the organizations which they serve, due to increasing time pressures and a need to see a tangible impact as a result of their efforts. Boomers and seniors, increasingly wealthy and able to ease up on their driven life-styles, will spend more of their free time engaged in social and political activism.

The causes that will energize the population will relate to environmental protection, drunk driving, crime and punishment and abortion. The driving force behind involvement in these matters will be personal gain, such as having valued relationships, ensuring a safer and healthier world in which to live and reducing the emotional stress caused by these national dilemmas. While involvement in these movements may appear to be altruistic, the underlying motivations will, more often than not, be self-centered.

Malls, the current rage for shopping and for socializing among young people, will lose their social magnetism. (They are likely to keep their status as dominant dens of consumption.) One of the substitutes will be large, outdoor community events. The purpose of these events will be to allow people to celebrate some R&R: roots and relationships. For a people seeking to feel a sense of connectedness and stability, being at such a local event will serve as a first blush at creating a sense of belonging.

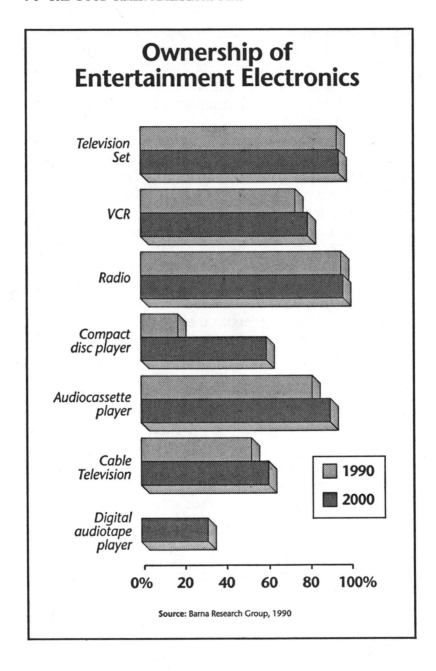

Ownership of Entertainment Electronics

Television Set

VCR

Radio

Compact disc player

Audiocassette player

Cable Television

1990
2000

Digital audiotape player

0% 20 40 60 80 100%

Source: Barna Research Group, 1990

More and More Media

We also expect people to spend increased amounts of time consuming mass media. This will partly be a function of the increased penetration of some existing forms of entertainment. For instance, cable television will grow from its current presence in 53 percent of American households, to about 60 percent by 2000. More than a dozen new cable channels will be introduced during the '90s. Most of the basic cable channels will commit large sums of money to producing original programming, to entice even more viewers away from the network offerings. Pay-per-view television, enabling viewers to watch recent movies or live special events, will also expand in popularity, increasing its total revenues by as much as seven times over their current volume.

An entirely new approach to broadcasting, called high definition television (HDTV), may also be on the market by 2000. Using higher resolution transmission and reception technologies, HDTV will require America to be totally refitted for television: new TV sets for consumers, as well as new broadcast equipment for stations. While many analysts are keen on the future of HDTV, there remains reason to doubt people's willingness to invest substantial sums in replacing equipment that already satisfies most people's standards.

VCRs, now found in about 75 percent of households, will be in about 80 percent by 2000. Compact disc players, which have already changed the face of the music industry, will continue to proliferate, jumping from their 12 percent penetration level in 1990 to more than 60 percent in 2000. Along the way, expect to see music companies totally phase out record albums. You can also anticipate the introduction of a new audio tape format, called digital audiotape. A cleaner, higher quality format, it will also go a long way toward improving music products available to the consumer, and open an entirely new industry for products.

Advances in technology will also change our involvement

with the media. One change that will revolutionize television is interactive programming. Systems are now being tested which will enable viewers, as they are watching the program, to dictate a TV story's plot from a group of choices. Other interactive systems will allow viewers to determine the scheduling of programs on certain channels, or to actually participate in game shows as they are being broadcast. These changes will alter our viewing from passive to active involvement, and enable us to exercise greater creativity and control in our entertainment environment.

Among the less high tech media, reading for pleasure will remain a favorite pastime, as Boomers hold steady their spending for books and magazines. The boom in sales of children's books that made the late '80s lucrative for many publishers, however, will tail off by 1996. Book sales may be enhanced by the introduction of interactive computer software that will enable readers to participate in the unfolding of the plot in books of fiction. It is also likely that publishers will produce electronic nonfictional works which respond to the particular interests and questions of readers, providing a more conversational experience through the computer and the book text.

Professional sports will surge in popularity, with the addition of more teams around the nation's cities. Perking people's interests will be the introduction of international competition into the existing leagues. More states may well legalize gambling, arguing its value and legitimacy on the basis of the legalization of state lotteries.

✝ CHALLENGES AND OPPORTUNITIES FOR THE CHURCH

As society changes, the Church must adapt accordingly. Even is areas such as leisure, the shifts described above must be reflected in how local congregations make Christianity come alive in people's lives. If nothing else, we must recognize that we are in a competitive environment. If we hope to include people in the life of the Church, we must provide appealing and high quality activities that can successfully compete for people's time, attention and resources.

Church programs should include more entertainment-related activities. Because Americans perceive Christian churches to

---

Let people know that you are in touch with their life-style, sensitive to their time needs and capable of providing relevant and enjoyable leisure experiences.

---

have a values filter through which all activities pass, many adults (especially those with children) will depend upon the Church to provide morally acceptable forms of entertainment—something which will be increasingly difficult to find in the '90s.

Vary the Menu

For churches to consistently garner attendance and involvement at events and programs, there must also be greater variety in what is offered. The American public has a low tolerance for repetition. Rotating successful programs will be more advantageous than using those programs on a long-term basis. Creativity in the development of new offerings will also strike a resonant chord with adults.

Acknowledge the fact that people are interested in short bursts of activity. Programs that feature teaching, sports, entertainment or other activities that last for hours on end will lose people quickly. The message that you send to people through the nature of your programs and events is important. Through the design of your extra-curricular programs, let them know that you are in touch with their life-style, sensitive to their time needs and capable of providing relevant and enjoyable leisure experiences.

Foster Relationships
Perhaps more than any other institution in America, the local church is poised to address people's need for more, and deeper relationships. As you create free time activities, try to achieve a balance between those which are individualized and those which facilitate interaction between people. Adults in the '90s will feel more comfortable with individualized activities, while harboring at the same time a desire for opportunities to connect with other, like-minded people, too.

Some churches have already seen the value of integrating people's felt needs and the development of church-sponsored activities. For example, a number of congregations have one hour sessions several days a week in which women can meet at the church for aerobic exercising or "jazzercize" classes. There will be growing opportunities to offer such programs for people. While these activities may not be overtly spiritual, they do fit with our calling to take care of our bodies, and it can be done in the presence of people with whom lasting relationships can be built.

Remember how the corner tavern used to be the place where the men of the neighborhood would congregate to watch major sports events, like the World Series or championship boxing matches? While times have changed, that same concept can still be used to great impact by the Church. Most churches have a large hall or auditorium which could be used for special gatherings built around major media events—sports, political debates, entertainment specials and the like.

Add to Perceived Value

It may not simply be enough, however, to have the event shown on a large-screen television in a gymnasium. Churches would profit from integrating the "value added" marketing concept which will be so common during the '90s. Value added marketing requires offering the basic product, then adding something special to it to enhance the perceived value, causing the product in the enhanced form to be more attractive than it would be otherwise.

Churches could make mass media events into a special church or community event. Remember: Americans want unique and special experiences. Surrounding an upcoming event with additional benefits (special speakers, musical entertainment, free materials, special comforts) for those who attend could draw people from all walks of life—including those who do not normally associate with churches. In the process, then, the Church develops a special image and becomes the social glue of the community—a glue that is increasingly absent in America's cities, suburbs and small towns.

With reading and the use of home computers and VCRs continuing to fill significant proportions of our spare time, consider the value of your church library. Is it simply a place where theological treatises collect dust? A number of forward-thinking churches have already converted their libraries into media centers, where church members can check out current books, videotapes, and even special types of computer software. Audiotapes are also available for loan. These churches have not merely accumulated tapes of the pastor's teaching, or books by renowned theologians. They have a variety of media that relate to the interests of the public. Their libraries are not simply a dumping grounds for scholarly books, but a treasure trove of exciting, contemporary and useful products.

Attract People with Causes
Finally, since churches rely heavily upon volunteers, we must keep in mind that during the '90s, sacrificing time to help the Church will rate as a lower priority to many people. We will become more cause-driven, responding to critical social and political issues. Can the Church portray the spiritual emptiness of many people's lives as an issue worth committing to? Can we create the aura of Christianity as a contemporary movement that is reshaping the value structure of America, after several decades of decadence and demise? Churches able to do such things will find a plentiful field of volunteers to call upon for various ministries. The key to maintaining those people will be the effective communication and celebration of the positive, tangible results of their efforts. The carrot at the end of the stick will be vivid demonstrations of the Church's impact on individual lives, the community, and our nation.

Notes
1. David Sheff, "Portrait of a Generation," *Rolling Stone,* May 5, 1988, pp. 46-65.
2. John P. Robinson, "Time for Work," *American Demographics,* April 1989, p. 68; and "Who's Doing the Housework," Ibid., December 1988.
3. Ibid.

6 THE BOTTOM LINE: JOBS, SPENDING AND TRADE

CHAPTER HIGHLIGHTS:

►Working women will gain greater pay, responsibility and prestige. The combined entry of women, minorities and immigrants into the work force in the '90s will account for 90 percent of the labor market expansion.

►America's economic center for the decade—either New York or Los Angeles—will be determined by the events unfolding in Europe, China and the Soviet Union.

►Home-based work will be three times as common in 2000.

►Boomers, too numerous for all to receive the job promotions desired, will change careers earlier and more often than their predecessors, redefining their occupational goals along the way.

►With the prospect of a major depression on the horizon, companies will invest more heavily in human capital, and may resort to hiring "electronic immigrants."

►Local churches will find that numerical growth requires "niche marketing" techniques and media.   ►►►►►

AS WE POINTED OUT IN CHAPTER 1, MONEY IS BEING REPLACED BY TIME as our most treasured and protected resource. However, Americans will still rely upon money to define how well they are doing. Whether we are scrutinizing household incomes and spending patterns, national budgets and business success or international trade deficits and commerce arrangements, financial standing remains the dominant means of discerning one's position, power and potential. With changes in household demographics, in attitudes and values and in the balance of world power and productivity, the coming decade will generate sweeping changes in our economic perspectives and practices.

AMERICA, 1990

The '80s wrought major shifts related to the presence of women in the labor force, the amount of time spent working, the acceleration in the number of people working from their homes and the frequency of cross-industry career transitions.

Women at Work

Women now constitute a major segment of the work force. An estimated 56 percent of women now work outside of their home, with roughly equal numbers of mothers and empty nesters holding down jobs. More importantly, women have caught the enterpreneurial spirit in a major way, now owning almost three out of every ten small businesses, and opening new small business operations five times more often than men. Women have made substantial advances in the traditional business community, as well. The earnings of women relative to that of men has climbed steadily: they now make roughly 70 percent the income of males. And their numbers are significantly increasing in executive positions and on corporate boards of directors.

Most women today work because they feel they need to in order to make ends meet. On the average, American households

---

In 1990, an estimated 6 million households have at least one head of the household using the home as a work base.

---

believe that they need $8,000-$11,000 more in annual income to live comfortably.[1] Although a majority of women say they would stop working if they did not have to, research indicates that once females enter the labor force they tend to remain working unless they bear children or reach retirement age.

New Patterns of Work
Meanwhile, the influx of new office technology at affordable prices has spawned a new work style: people working from their homes, either starting new businesses or working from the home at the request (and with the financial support) of their corporate employer. In 1980, few people worked from their home. Those who did usually ran day care centers or prepared mailings for marketing firms. In 1990, an estimated 6 million households have at least one head of the household using the home as a work base.

Not only have many people changed where they work, but more and more people are changing what they do for a living. In the undying search for meaning and fulfillment in life, millions of adults are jumping from one industry to another every year, seeking a more interesting or satisfying job experience. Many younger adults now exit from college with the *expectation* of changing industries every decade or so, in the quest for adventure, excitement and a change of scenery. The majority of changes are happening within the service sector of the economy, in which knowledge of a few basic technical skills, along with the ability to communicate effectively, enables such transitions to be made more easily.

People's attitudes toward charity and their own affluence are responsible for the increasing amounts of money Americans are giving to nonprofit organizations. During the '80s, there was a major swing from interest in helping people overseas to funding development and assistance projects within America. The "help America first" mentality resulted in record-breaking donations to organizations involved in medical research, educational projects and urban development and assistance activities.

Marketing and Morals

Also in response to the changing perception of self and our place in the world, marketing has undergone a seminal change. Leading companies are leaving mass marketing behind in favor of targeted or "niche" marketing. Using new technologies that enable them to pinpoint specific populations with the highest response potential, marketers are shifting their advertising dollars to those media which enable them to locate the population segments they wish to reach. This has resulted in different media gaining favor: direct mail, telemarketing, cable television, and point-of-purchase advertising are gaining increasing proportions of marketing budgets.

At the same time that corporations have reassigned their

marketing resources, the general public has refocused its attention on what they are doing, and how. Scandals in the business world have caused the public to examine the ethical behavior of corporate America. The antics of Ivan Boesky, Michael Milken and others have captured the fancy of the media, and made it fashionable to think about business ethics. Many investors have also begun to realign their portfolios out of ethi-

---

Some estimate that four out of five companies will offer their employees flexible time schedules—more than double the proportion who do so today.

---

cal considerations such as discrimination (South Africa), hiring practices (low wages) or their product effect (nuclear weaponry, products with negative environmental consequences).

Of East and West

The closing years of the '80s brought a tornado of change in the world, leaving our nation without a well-defined economic focus for the future. In the past, New York has been our economic center, based upon trade relationships with Europe. Today, however, the competition has heated up. The Pacific Rim economy, encompassing the nations in or bordering on the Pacific Ocean (Japan, Australia, Hong Kong, China, Southeast Asia), represents a rapidly growing marketplace which American corporations have found attractive. In dealing with the Pacific Rim, Los Angeles, rather than New York, serves as the economic core. Many economists believe that Los Angeles represents the heart of our economic future, given its strategic location, unique infrastructure and growing population. However, the recent restructuring of Eastern Europe and the Soviet Union, along with the approaching European Economic Community agreement scheduled to take effect in 1992, have created additional confusion regarding our economic focus.

AMERICA, 2000

You may anticipate some important changes in the next decade related to careers, personal finances and international economics.

Marketers are now bracing for the continuation of a massive shift in perspective by consumers. We will shy away from appeals based upon lowest price, in favor of products offering the best value. As an affluent and skeptical nation, we are coming to the conclusion that a bargain is not just an inexpensive product, but rather one which supplies the consumer with above-average value for the money spent. In the same way, employees will evaluate jobs differently. Beyond a minimum level of salary deemed necessary for living at a reasonable lifestyle level, people will seek assurances of fulfillment rather than large sums of money.

Women will continue to join the work force in ever-increasing numbers, and will make further gains toward equality with men in terms of pay and prestige. By 2000, more than 60 percent of all working-aged females will be employed. In fact, the new workers of the '90s will barely resemble the traditional labor force. White, native-born males will represent just 10 percent of the growth in the labor force during the '90s. The remainder will come from women, immigrants and minorities.[2]

Financially, the Rand Corporation projects that by 2000

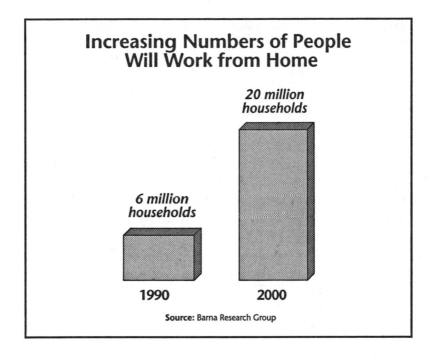

Increasing Numbers of People Will Work from Home

20 million households

6 million households

1990   2000

Source: Barna Research Group

women will be earning 80 percent as much as men. These gains will not come without a price, of course, as women will bring to the labor force better educational backgrounds, increased levels of experience and greater responsibility within corporations. These heightened rewards and responsibilities will create greater tension and conflict within families, increased chances of divorce and smaller families.

The work environment itself will be a different place, too. Forty percent of all the new jobs created by the turn of the century will require higher skill levels than today's average job. Hours are less likely to be 9-to-5, with the increase in 24-hour services and weekend work. Some estimate that four out of five companies will offer their employees flexible time schedules (that's more than double the proportion who do so today). Employers will be more concerned about the completion of specified tasks and the quality of people's work than the number of hours logged by employees.

Normally, as people age, they are likely to stick with their job longer. The difficulty of finding another position at higher salary levels, and one that does not require uprooting the family from house, friends and community ties, causes older employees to be more stable. Boomers, however, present a unique situation. Because there are so many people in that generation, there will simply not be enough executive positions to go around. Consequently, job hopping, even among many older adults, will be common. Along the way, many Boomers will pause to reconsider their definition of success. A generation unwilling to accept failure, Boomers will restructure their attitudes about occupational goals and upward career mobility toward softening the blow of stunted career growth.

In the process of reexamining what is important, millions of Boomers will switch to a new career. By 2000, the average adult will make four to six career changes during his or her lifetime. To prepare for those transitions, many will commit their free time to educational programs geared to retraining in anticipation of a career jump.

Companies will respond to the changes in the marketplace with a number of creative and technological innovations. For one, more and more people will be sent home to conduct their work. Some companies will establish a hybrid strategy, with employees working at home for a portion of the week, and commuting to a smaller, less imposing satellite office for part of the week. More corporations will be leaving their high-rent offices in downtown skyscrapers, realizing the financial savings and reduced stress levels made possible by reliance on an in-home labor force. By 2000, as many as 20 million individuals may be working from their homes, either on behalf of their employer or as self-employed workers. More homes, therefore, will be equipped with personal computers, desktop copiers and fax machines.

Companies relying upon people to do high-tech tasks on computers may resort to hiring "electronic immigrants." These organizations will hire technically skilled people in foreign countries where the cost of skilled labor is substantially lower than in the United States. Those employees will work from their home, or a central office area in their community, and

---

Many corporations will learn that the aggressive leveraged buyouts and hostile takeovers of the '80s was unwarranted.

"telecommute"—that is, send their work to the main office in America via computer modems. You can bet that this arrangement, a financial bonanza for American-based firms, will raise major political issues and debate regarding the loss of jobs to foreign markets, and the involvement of foreign nations in the development of American technology.

One of the major pushes of American corporations during the '90s will be the development of human capital. For the past few decades, we have emphasized the development of physical capital—new manufacturing facilities, advanced electronics, etc. Even our business schools have concentrated on instilling capabilities related to number crunching rather than relating to other people. By 2000, expect to see new curricula in our business schools and major investments by corporations in employee training programs that teach new skills, especially those related to communication and literacy.

The '80s also gave birth to corporate aggressiveness, as leveraged buyouts and hostile takeovers consistently filled the business news. As the '90s progress, many corporations will learn that the greed which stimulated such actions was unwarranted. They will experience severe problems with the blending of corporate cultures, the efficiency of new organizational structures and low productivity resulting from lack of insight into the new business categories in which they suddenly were operating. More profits from these newly configured corporations will be pumped into legal protection against future hostile takeovers, and into attempts to develop a workable structure. Expect to see fewer hostile takeovers in the next decade, and to see many of those which occurred during the '80s dissolved through the break-up of conglomerates.

Nationally, many experts forecast a major economic collapse for the early '90s, with 1991-92 mentioned most often as the likely period of the decline. Some of the more conservative economists are predicting a depression, while others expect only a recession. These people point to a variety of factors that could lead to such economic turbulence: decreasing levels of investment, minimal personal savings, rising foreign investment in the U.S., an increasing trade deficit (which may reach $1 trillion by 2000—we are already the world's biggest debtor), the widening gap between the rich and the poor and inadequate investment in modernization. While it would be mere speculation to assert with confidence that such a collapse is likely, the signs of bad economic health are evident, and require serious response if the national economy is to weather the turbulent times ahead.[3]

It is likely that we will have a shakeout of the service sector of the economy. We are likely to find businesses investing more heavily in automation. Rather than pioneering advances in technology, we will concentrate upon applications of the new technologies developed in the past decade. These applications will lead to enhanced productivity, and make America more competitive in the global market.

✝ CHALLENGES AND OPPORTUNITIES FOR THE CHURCH

Building up the numbers of people associated with the local church will require churches to utilize niche marketing strategies. Thanks to the application of single-source and relational databases, Americans will be used to receiving persuasive communications that acknowledge their personal background, experiences and interests.

If the local church continues to rely upon mass advertising campaigns, via media such as the newspaper, the chances are strong that most people will remain unaware of the campaigns, or ignore them because they are not in step with the times. Even in promoting events and programs within the Church, we must respect people's time and uniqueness enough to communicate in ways that are currently practiced and are relevant to the individual.

The local church might also study options for providing special training programs for its people. With high levels of transience, frequent career changes and a national movement to upgrade technical skills and functional literacy, America will be in a training mode. The Church can sponsor programs to benefit from this openness to training.

One area in which many church people will need to be trained is stewardship. While church leaders and clergy typically assume that the congregation understands its responsibility regarding church financial support, the research suggests otherwise. As Boomers become active in the Church, they may be especially difficult to stimulate to significant giving levels. They will already be donating money to a variety of nonprofit organizations. Giving to a church will not be viewed as a priority — unless the church works diligently and intelligently to lead them to lift it to higher priority. They will have to see tangible and moving results of such support. Because most Boomers will not think of themselves as affluent, they need to understand the principles of stewardship described in Scripture.

While the people of the Church, as well as the organization itself, should always behave in ways that are beyond reproach, expect even stricter scrutiny in the days ahead. As ethics becomes a standard topic of discussion and consideration, churches will be watched at all times. Further, political pressure will be put on the government to monitor the financial operations of churches. Modeling ethical behavior will have an even greater impact than teaching on the subject.

Communicating with volunteers and members may take on new forms, as more people work from their homes and have equipment such as modems and fax machines at home. People will feel the crunch of time pressure due to owning small businesses (the proportion will rise significantly in the next decade), living in homes with all adults employed and having new responsibilities such as caring for the elderly. "Time is money" will be even more meaningful to people. Volunteer time will be scarcer to come by, and must be used efficiently.

Finally, although there is no guarantee that a depression will hit America, it may be worthwhile to consider how both individuals and local churches would respond to a major economic collapse. Preparing programs and policies, and perhaps even developing a reserve resource base that will be useful in such a situation, might be a sensible strategy to pursue.

Notes
1. "Tracking Tomorrow's Trends," *USA Today*, 1986, p. 6.
2. "The Next Challenge," *Business Week*, Sept. 25, 1989, p. 242.
3. Joe Cappo, "Future Scope," (Chicago: Longman Financial Services, 1990), pp. 86-87. See also "Innovation in America," special report, *Business Week*, 1989.

PART III
CHANGES IN PATTERNS OF FAITH

By 2000, less than half of our adult population will say that religion is very important in their daily lives. Less than 40 percent will even associate themselves with a Protestant denomination.

7 RELIGIOUS BELIEF AND INVOLVEMENT

CHAPTER HIGHLIGHTS:

▶Although Americans generally possess orthodox beliefs about God, Christ and Satan, the momentum is against integrating spiritual belief with daily behavior.

▶The window of opportunity for reaching Americans with the gospel appears to be closing rapidly.

▶The '90s promise to bring a move toward syncretism—the blending of the most popular aspects of Christianity with similarly pleasing elements from other religious traditions.

▶Christians not only have to live as examples of the faith; we will be challenged to show how faith is not simply a religious proposition, but a basis for life-style and purpose.

▶The Body of Christ must be awakened to the spiritual crisis we face, and to the need for the discipling of believers by fellow believers, for the purposes of growth and accountability. ▶▶▶▶▶

AMERICA HAS A STRONG RELIGIOUS HERITAGE. OVER THE PAST 200 years, we have been recognized as a world leader in the Christian faith, while allowing for a diversity of personal beliefs and religious practices apart from that tradition. As we enter the '90s, the major upheavals occurring around the globe are creating a renewed interest in religious freedom and practice. America, too, is undergoing significant changes regarding its religious beliefs and participation.

 AMERICA, 1990

Most Americans are exposed to information about religion every day. Through radio, television, newspapers and magazines, books and private conversation, religion remains a topic very much alive and in the consciousness of the population.

However, we have begun to witness a decline in the religious attentiveness of adults. In 1987, nearly six out of ten adults said that religion was very important in their everyday lives. That proportion has consistently dropped since then. Similarly, whereas almost three out of four adults described themselves as "religious" in 1986, just three out of five adults make the same claim today. The indications are that the window of opportunity for evangelism, which was wide open during the early and mid-'80s, is rapidly closing.

We "Say, and Do Not"
Due largely to family heritage and a broad understanding of the Christian faith, most Americans—about four out of five—describe themselves as "Christian." That term means

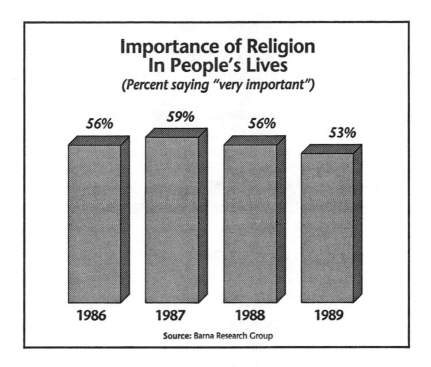

**Importance of Religion
In People's Lives**
(Percent saying "very important")

56%   59%   56%   53%

1986   1987   1988   1989

Source: Barna Research Group

many things to many people. Amazingly, only about one out of every five individuals say Christianity has to do with the acceptance of, or a personal relationship with Jesus Christ. Many more people associate being a Christian with life-styles and behavior: loving other people, helping others, being a good person, etc. Some equate the term with a general belief in God. Still others say it has to do with religious practices such as attending church or "being religious". In other words, the concept of being a Christian has become bland and generic. Much of the spiritual dimension of the concept has been lost while the population has been immunized to the Christian faith.

There is an interesting contradiction, too, between what most of us say we believe and what we do (or don't do) in response to those beliefs. The vast majority of Americans have orthodox Christian beliefs: they acknowledge the virgin birth,

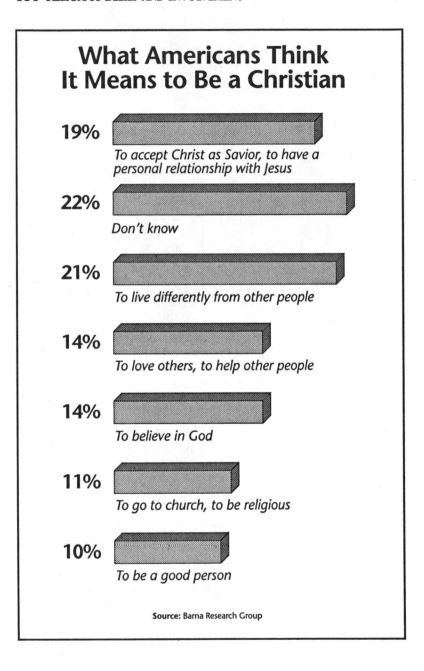

What Americans Think It Means to Be a Christian

19% To accept Christ as Savior, to have a personal relationship with Jesus

22% Don't know

21% To live differently from other people

14% To love others, to help other people

14% To believe in God

11% To go to church, to be religious

10% To be a good person

Source: Barna Research Group

the death and resurrection of Jesus Christ, the power of prayer, the reality of miracles by God, the importance of the Church, the reality of Satan and hell and the life of the Holy Spirit in believers. More than nine out of ten adults own a Bible, and a majority of them even believe that it is God's written word, totally accurate in its teaching. Perhaps surprisingly, a majority of American adults—about three out of five—claim that they have made a personal commitment to Jesus Christ that is still important in their lives today.

But our actions indicate that our beliefs are not held to be significant enough to share them with others. In the past seven years, the proportion of adults who have accepted Jesus Christ as their personal Savior (34 percent) has not increased. Church attendance remains steady, although lower than three decades ago (less than half of all adults attend church on any given Sunday). Loyalty to the Church, as an institution in which we have a personal investment and which we care about, is dropping. Attendance in adult Sunday School classes is diminishing. Membership in Christian churches is waning. Involvement in small group Bible studies has not increased in several years. Willingness to assume a leadership role in the congregation is declining. Time spent in Bible reading and Bible study has remained constant—and at a minimal level—for the past seven years.

Some social analysts have argued that the televangelism scandals of the late '80s initiated a downward tumble for Christianity that has yet to be halted. The data, however, do not support this theory. The evidence does indicate that the Jim Bakker and Jimmy Swaggart episodes, in particular, confirmed some negative feelings that many adults previously held about the Christian Church. But there has been no enduring determination to judge either the faith in general or local churches in particular on the basis of those circumstances.

The place of the Bible in America is worth further evalua-

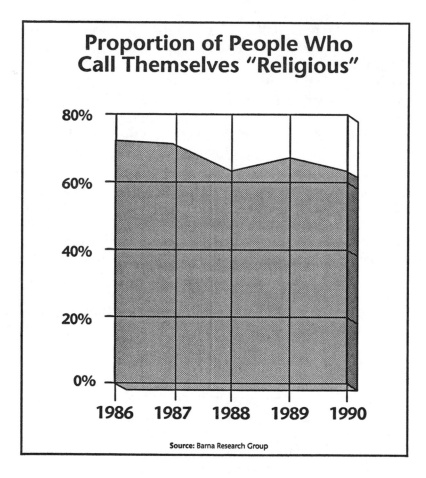

Proportion of People Who Call Themselves "Religious"

Source: Barna Research Group

tion. It is revered as "the good book," and is found in most homes across the country. Yet, less than half of America will open that book during the week. Those who do read it during the week do not make the Bible a priority: they spend more time on almost every leisure or other activity in which they engage than they do reading Scripture. Studies show that we have become a nation of biblical illiterates, lacking knowledge of what is in the Bible, and showing limited commitment to applying its truths to our daily behavior.

The Forecast: Mostly Cloudy

Attitudes about the value of the Christian faith are also deteriorating slowly but steadily. A large minority of adults say that the Church is not "relevant" for today. The majority of adults say that in difficult times they will put their trust in self rather than in God. Less than half of the public believes that churches and religious faith can help people deal with difficult times in their life.

One outgrowth of this situation is that people are increasingly private about their religious faith. Substantial proportions of Americans justify their reticence to engage in religious discussion or "proselytizing" by suggesting that evangelism is the job of the professional clergy and media evangelists; that we ought to respect the separation of church and state; that discussing religion only leads to controversy and dissension; and that religion is too personal a matter to openly discuss. Further, because millions of Christians who do share their faith with others emerge from those experiences feeling that they have failed, increasing numbers of well-intentioned believers have a vested interest in perceiving evangelism to be the job of the institutional church or of those people who have formal education in theology and evangelism.

AMERICA, 2000

We are in for a rough ride in the decade ahead. The trends suggest that the importance of religion in people's life will continue its slow decline. By 2000, less than half of our adult population will say that religion is very important in their daily lives. For millions of Americans, religion will simply refer to a series of Sunday morning rituals that a shrinking number of traditionalists play. Less than 40 percent of the population will even associate themselves with a Protestant denomination. Barely

The Bible in America

Use of the Bible:

■ 93% of all households own one or more Bible(s)

■ 12% of adults read the Bible every day

■ 57% of adults do not read the Bible at all during a typical week

■ Among Bible readers, the average time spent reading the Bible is 65 minutes a week

■ 38% say that they often turn to the Bible for help or encouragement.

Perceptions of the Bible:

■ 31% of all adults say the Bible is too difficult to understand

■ 42% of American adults do not agree that "the Bible is the written word of God, and is totally accurate in all that it teaches."

Knowledge of the Bible:

■ 31% knew that the expression "God helps those who help themselves" is *not* in the Bible

■ 52% correctly stated that the book of Thomas is *not* part of the Bible

■ Only 48% knew that the book of Jonah is in the Bible

■ 58% did not know who preached the Sermon on the Mount.

Source: Barna Research Group

one out of three adults will include church attendance on their list of things to do on Sundays.

This situation is all the more disturbing because, by all rights, 2000 should provide a reasonably optimistic picture for the Christian faith. Boomers will have matured to ages at which people generally become more stable, more serious and more interested in spiritual matters. We know that the Boomers, even more than most generations, have searched intensely for years in an attempt to understand their purpose in life. As most of them are still seeking answers to their fundamental questions of purpose and meaning, the Church should arise as a reasonable solution to their dilemma. Yet, this is not likely to be the case.

On the other hand, research consistently shows that people are most likely to accept Christ as their Savior before they reach the age of 18. Currently, about two-thirds of all decisions for Christ happen by that age. The demographic curves, however, point out that we will have a declining pool of young people to reach as the decade unfolds.

What We Likely Won't Do
Why won't Christianity transform Americans in the '90s?

Realize that Americans most readily accept institutions, philosophies, programs or individuals that respond to our felt needs through highly personalized and relevant messages. We are looking for that which is fresh and exciting, but credible and substantive. We are interested in that which is solid but flexible. The Christian faith, as promoted in our churches today, offers few of these traits.

The '80s were a decade in which millions of young adults gave the Church another chance. But relatively few found much that was of perceived value, and the majority have again turned their backs on the Church, perhaps permanently.

The Church will continue to emphasize aspects which are of little importance or meaning to the common person. For instance, some church leaders will recognize that congregations that grow are those in which a significant worship time is provided each Sunday. There will be a rush to imitate those churches, in the belief that pushing worship is the key to growth.

The fact is that most young adults have no concept of worship. One study showed that Boomers who are lay leaders in their churches have only a vague notion of what real worship is about, and that what their churches do in the realm of worship has little to do with their commitment to a church.

More generally, adults will also find the call to sacrifice, obedience and selflessness to be out of line with their own direction in life. The commands of Jesus will seem like an appeal to asceticism to most Americans, an unappealing prospect at best. In an era in which we are seeking to build our self-esteem and to feel good about ourselves through conscious, overt acts of generosity and kindness, the hardline requirements of Christianity, will simply be too much for millions of people to accept. They may not vociferously challenge or oppose the Christian life-style and belief structure, but they will dismiss our faith as impractical and unreasonable for today's world.

At the same time, one of the more hopeful signs is that the renewal expected to blossom throughout Eastern Europe and the Soviet Union, and which is likely to continue throughout Southeast Asia, South America and Africa, may direct people's attention to the significant events happening in those areas. However, for those international explosions of faith to be translated into any meaningful reaction in America, our local churches must be prepared to convert that intrigue into something deeper. It does not appear that many churches in the U.S. are poised to do so, nor that many churches will move in the direction of doing anything more than rejoicing over the spiritual growth in other nations.

What Many Had Rather Believe

Left to their own devices, adults will be less impressed by, and less accepting of, Christianity's most basic and important beliefs. Instead, as adults continue their search for truth and purpose, they will become syncretistic. Syncretism was a form of religion developed many centuries ago, in which people

---

Most Christians do not perceive the Church to be in the midst of the most severe struggle it has faced in centuries.

---

took the best facets of each religion they encountered and formed a new, blended faith. As elements of Eastern religions become more prolific, the most appealing aspects of Christianity (which will be the life-style elements, rather than the central spiritual tenets) will be wed to the exotic and fascinating attributes of eastern faiths. The result will be a people who honestly believe that they have improved Christianity, and who would even consider themselves to be Christian, despite their creative restructuring of the faith.

This synthetic religion will coincide with the philosophic bent of the nation. By 2000, Americans will be even less interested in absolutes, preferring those perspectives which allow for relative values to gain credence. Casting issues in a black-and-white mode will disgust many people, since they will cling to the notion that there is no absolute truth, no absolute reality and no absolute force. Even our understanding of God is in the process of being reshaped due to this acceptance of conditional truth.

A decade from now, increasing numbers of Americans will think of God not as the singular, all-powerful Being who created and rules the universe, but as a general and impersonal power. In 2000, most Americans will no longer assume that your God is my God, and that the God of the Christian Church is the only God in existence. Those who feared the takeover of communism railed against the dangers of America becoming a godless nation. They need not fear: we will become just the opposite, a nation filled with many gods.

Quality Concerns

In the midst of this spiritual decay, it is likely that "the remnant" (i.e., the portion of the population dedicated to following Christ) will remain intact. The proportion of born-again Christians should remain in the 30-35 percent range. The greatest danger comes, however, not in the quantity of Christians but in the *quality* of their witness.

Most Christians will live oblivious to the spiritual crisis of America. They will live as if all were well, and will demonstrate a decreasing intensity of commitment to the work of the Church. Faced with growing numbers of options for their time and loyalty, Christians will generally make the Church just one of many pressing priorities. Because of their own insecurities about promoting their faith, they will share their beliefs with others less frequently. They will get involved in church activities less often. Sensitive to the unsatisfactory quality of leadership they experience within the Church, and the untenable quality of programs and services offered by most congregations, they will be less likely to closely associate with the Church.

Personally, people will spend even less time in prayer and Bible study than they do today. While we might expect Bible ownership to remain high, and attendance at children's Sunday School to show some strength, the adult population will largely be impervious to attempts to deepen their faith.

✝ CHALLENGES AND OPPORTUNITIES TO THE CHURCH

The first challenge we must rise to meet is the need to awaken the Christian community to America's spiritual crisis. Incredibly, most Christians do not perceive the Church to be in the midst of the most severe struggle it has faced in centuries. Perhaps we have simply become accustomed to hearing gloom and doom preaching, or reading books about the impending decline of civilization. Just as the general public have been anesthetized to the gospel, maybe we have been inoculated against cries alerting us to the present danger.

The encouraging realization is that Americans characteristically respond to a good fight. In the '90s, as we seek adventure and excitement, if the Church positions the nature of our crisis properly, and works intelligently toward arming the people for the battles ahead, this could be an exciting decade of response to the threat of the Enemy.

Don't Downplay Discipleship

One of the glaring weaknesses of the Church has been in the area of discipling and accountability. If we are to make inroads during these next 10 years, we must support each other in deeper, more personal ways. While we may feel threatened by the vulnerability of confession, learning, and sharing needs, there seems to be little chance that the Body can be strengthened sufficiently to progress without the discipline of discipleship.

We will be tempted to downplay the importance of commitment and obedience. We will be tempted to soften the truth so that a hardened generation will give us a fair hearing. There is a fine line between clever marketing and compromised spirituality.

Does this mean we should not attempt to repackage the gospel in ways that may be more attractive to nonbelievers? No! We *must* do so if we hope to get our message to emerge from the flood of commercial messages that are directed at us each day. Our goal, however, must be to describe the faith in ways which are clearly relevant to today's circumstances and tensions, but without minimizing the hard truths that Jesus taught and demands of us. In a society that does not recognize absolutes, we must make absolutes seem not only relevant but natural and appealing.

Explain the Basics—Relevantly

In approaching the public, let's not base our words and actions on unfounded assumptions. We tend to think that everyone knows the basics, that they understand how the Christian faith works and why they ought to accept Christ. All that's needed, we reason, is a push in the right direction. Unfortunately, the research shows that while people may have some "head knowledge" related to the faith, they have insufficient context to comprehend what the beliefs they have learned have to do with day-to-day reality. Even on matters which, from our perspective, are clearly explained in the Bible, there is much misunderstanding and ignorance about basic scriptural principles.

Thus, we cannot assume that when we urge people to pray, they know what that means. Similarly, when we encourage people to engage in meaningful worship or Bible study we cannot afford to let our assumptions dictate our actions and expectations. Even on matters of knowledge, the research indicates that while people may use concepts such as "sin" or "the Trinity" in polite conversation, they have little idea how those concepts fit into a deeper spiritual perspective.

To communicate clearly and effectively, we must be certain that everyone understands what we mean when we use such concepts, and how we can incorporate those concepts into a substantive and invigorating faith. The '90s represent an ideal time for us to reinforce the basic aspects of our faith, emphasizing the application of such knowledge to a new mode of behavior and thought that reflects Jesus.

One step in this direction would be to recast the prevailing perspective about our faith. During the '90s, positioning Christianity as a "religion" may do us more harm than good. This approach simply encourages people to categorize the elements

---

If we expand people's concept of Christianity so they view it as a life-style and a purpose, rather than a theology, perhaps we would challenge them to take our faith more seriously.

---

of our faith as one among several "religious" options, and thereby limit the influence of Christian principles and teaching to the religious sphere of life. This enables people to isolate the truths and demands of the faith from the reality of every other dimension of their existence. Christianity can be neatly boxed and laid aside, as long as it is nothing more than a series of proverbs and teachings about man, God, life, eternity and the like.

Doing the Faith

If, however, we expand people's concept of Christianity so they view it as a life-style and a purpose, rather than as a theology, perhaps we would challenge them to take our faith more seriously. To a great extent, we will be taken only as seriously as we expect people to take us. If we can help the world to recognize that our faith is not a one dimensional experience, but is a multi-faceted way of life which permeates every thought, action and experience, Christianity would not only assume greater importance in the minds of people, but would challenge non-believers to explore this faith in a new way.

This means we will have to demonstrate the relevance of Christianity in every dimension of our lives. We cannot be Sunday Christians. More emphasis must be placed upon why we believe and how we live those beliefs. As Americans grow increasingly hardened and skeptical, the built-in credibility of Christianity will be steadily reduced in people's minds. Christians must communicate the importance of the faith by exhibiting a life-style based upon a Christian philosophy of life. We have to convey our perception that the difference we make in the world is personally fulfilling, but achieved for the benefit of others, not ourselves. In short, we must be representatives of Christ through more than just the words we speak. Compassion, joy and a sense of mission must shine through us as often as possible.

Strategic Use of Word and Works
The way we use the Bible might also be reexamined to achieve maximum impact. The Word can become more accessible to people, and therefore more likely to be incorporated into people's lives. Preaching based upon the Bible can use people's felt needs as the hook to grab their attention. Generally speaking, sermons which expound on Scripture without a clear relationship to people's felt needs will fall upon deaf ears. The main interest of people who attend churches is in practical applications of the faith to their life. Thus, we have to enable people to use the Bible more effectively toward developing solutions to everyday problems. Even simple changes such as using modern translations or versions of the Bible help to remove the barrier between Scripture and today's adult.

In developing strategies for reaching the public, we may also wish to explore our resource allocation. Traditionally, we pour the bulk of our funds for outreach and evangelism into ministry to adults. Existing research shows that most people accept Christ before they become adults. With the population aging, and with fewer and fewer young adults to reach, we may wish to make a concerted effort at reaching adolescents during the coming decade. If we are striving to efficiently utilize limited resources, we may find that this represents our best approach to evangelistic outreach.

Learning from Overseas Successes

As the Church blossoms in other nations, we should have a plan for how we can position ourselves as a part of that growth. Creative approaches to informing, celebrating, assisting and studying what is happening with the Church abroad are necessary.

In fact, because the Church in America will lose its standing as the leader in worldwide Christianity, we would be wise to develop strategies that help us not only accept our loss of leadership, but to see that new standing as cause to rejoice and as a challenge for the future. Americans are accustomed to being the biggest or the best. Often, especially among Boomers, being second best is untenable. We have a responsibility, as leaders of the Church, to pave the way to handling our changing position in the worldwide community of believers with grace and excitement.

Each of us ought to take time to reflect on the significance of the explosive growth of the Church overseas. We should think through what we can do to make that situation more significant in our own lives. The cumulative effect of the resulting ideas, and the concentration of energy devoted to those programs and other activities could greatly enhance the development of both our personal spiritual development, and that of our local churches.

8 BODY LIFE: THE CHURCH AND SPIRITUALITY

CHAPTER HIGHLIGHTS:

▶Although the present number of Protestant churches—325,000—will swell to about 375,000 in the '90s, both church attendance and church membership will decline.

▶The fastest-growing religious groups in America will be non-Christian: Mormonism, Islam, Buddhism and new age sects.

▶Since many will continue to think of the Church as irrelevant, they will create their own systems of religious belief—synthetic faiths blending the "best" of various religions.

▶Loyalty to churches will decline. Among adults, one in four may attend several churches instead of identifying only one as their "church home."

▶The number of women in the clergy will double by the year 2000.   ▶▶▶▶▶

THE MOST COMMON WAY TO JUDGE THE HEALTH OF CHRISTIANITY IS to examine the vitality of local Churches. The most visible impact of the faith is seen at the congregational level. It is through the corporate practice of the faith that observers gain their clearest notion of what the Christian faith is about. And through the practice of Christianity in the congregational context, believers receive their greatest encouragement, edification and equipping for continued personal growth and ministry. Although recent years have brought renewed challenges to the role and viability of the church in American society, it remains one of our more durable and significant social institutions.

 AMERICA, 1990

Whatever barriers and difficulties may face the Church today, having enough local churches is not the issue. There are more than 150 Protestant denominations, and some 325,000 local congregations. There are an additional 23,000 Roman Catholic churches in America.[1] We have one Protestant church for every 550 adults in America—a better ratio of adults per franchise (if you'll pardon the analogy) than McDonald's, Sears, Domino's Pizza or even the U.S. Post Office can boast.

Our research tells us, though, that despite the quantity of churches in our midst, they go largely unnoticed by most people. The name recognition of the average church is lower than might be expected. Fewer than one out of every five people, on the average, are aware of the existence of the typical church located within their community.

Number of Protestant Churches by Denomination
(3,000 or more churches)

Southern Baptist Convention	34,717
Seventh Day Adventist	5,619
United Methodist	41,279
Evangelical Lutheran Church	10,269
Presbyterian Church (USA)	12,321
United Church of Christ	7,027
Assemblies of God	11,746
Episcopal	8,130
Christian/Church of Christ	5,627
Church of the Nazarene	5,384
American Baptist Church	4,277
Lutheran Church, Missouri Synod	4,884
National Baptist Convention, USA	3,205
Church of God, Cleveland	3,842
Church of God in Christ	3,939
Disciples of Christ	3,768

Source: "Churches in America as of February 1990," American Church Lists, Arlington, TX.

Attendance Patterns

During the course of this year, about 125 million adults will attend a church service, other than for a special occasion (such as a wedding, funeral or holiday service). On any given Sunday morning, about four out of ten adults will attend a church service, with Catholics slightly more likely than Protestants to do so. However, it is not the same four out of ten who attend church each week. Of those who attend a church service, about half say they attend every week, while one-quarter attend at least once a month, and the remaining one-quarter attend less frequently.

Number of Members per Denomination
(Data shown in thousands of members)

Denomination	1950	1960	1970	1980	1990	2000
Assemblies of God	318	509	625	1,064	2,478	2,663
Disciples of Christ	1,768	1,802	1,424	1,178	1,084	899
Episcopal	2,417	3,269	3,286	2,786	2,047	1,587
Evangelical Lutheran*	3,983	5,295	5,650	5,384	5,269	5,112
Lutheran, Missouri Synod	1,675	2,391	2,789	2,625	2,608	2,504
Presbyterian (PCUSA)*	3,211	4,162	4,045	3,362	2,798	2,234
Roman Catholic	28,635	42,105	48,215	50,450	54,972	59,889
Southern Baptist Conv.	7,080	9,732	11,628	13,600	15,202	16,802
United Church of Christ	1,977	2,241	1,960	1,736	1,689	1,525
United Methodist	9,653	10,641	10,509	9,519	8,973	8,265

* denotes combination of members from merged bodies.

Sources:
1950-1980 from *Yearbook of American and Canadian Churches, 1989*, Constant Jacquet, Jr., ed. (Nashville: Abingdon Publishing Co., 1989)
1990-2000 from projections from Barna Research Group, 1990.

The trend regarding Sunday School involvement is little different. The late '80s brought a surge in children's attendance, as Boomers enrolled their children in Sunday School classes in the hope of getting some help in raising their youngsters. Many Boomer parents believed that while religion was not something that they would benefit from at their current stage of life, religious instruction and exposure might inculcate some positive social values in their children which they, as parents, might have a difficult time instilling. Although what the Church has to offer is viewed by many of these parents as valuable for their children, they personally reject the notion that Sunday School classes would provide them with benefits commensurate with the effort involved in attending.

Attending Isn't Belonging

It is also important not to confuse participation in church events with church membership. The trends indicate that attendance has remained relatively stable during the past 20 years. Not so for membership. As the elderly pass away, they are being replaced in the Church by generations who have less loyalty to religion, to denominations, to the local churches with which they affiliate and to the very notion of being a formal member of a church.

In the '50s and '60s, membership was an overt indication of belonging to the community and being a solid citizen. Church membership has negative connotations today. People perceive it to be restrictive and to provide few benefits. Interestingly, although 84 percent say that being a member of a church is important, barely half of American adults are members of a church. In other words, the average adult thinks that belonging to a church is good for other people but represents unnecessary bondage and baggage for himself.

The decline in church membership has been occurring for the past decade. Between 1980 and 1990, seven of the nation's

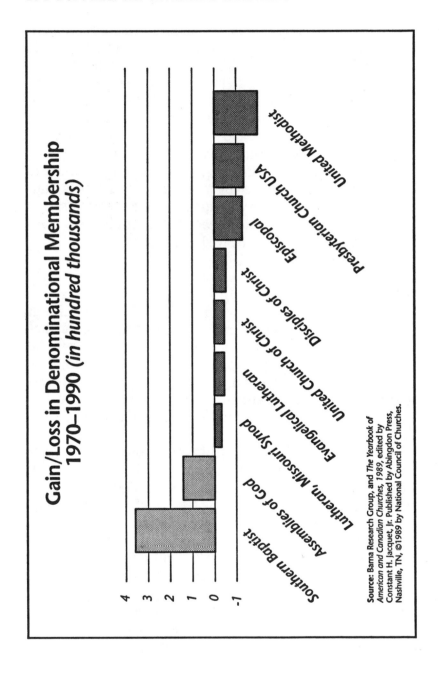

Gain/Loss in Denominational Membership
1970–1990 (in hundred thousands)

Source: Barna Research Group, and *The Yearbook of American and Canadian Churches, 1989*, edited by Constant H. Jacquet, Jr. Published by Abingdon Press, Nashville, TN, ©1989 by National Council of Churches.

nine largest denominations experienced membership declines. The only two that grew—the Southern Baptist Convention and Assemblies of God—were no match for the percentage growth experienced by the fastest growing religious bodies in America: the Mormon church, the Roman Catholic church, Buddhism, Islam and various New Age churches.

Giving Is Up, Evangelism Down

We cannot make the argument that we were underfunded, either. In 1989, Americans donated more than $50 billion to churches, with the vast majority of that money going to Protestant churches. In addition, more than $10 billion worth of time was donated by church volunteers for the work of local churches.

Some question the way in which we spend our money. One study showed that while most churches believe they are in business to spread the gospel, they actually spend very little money on such activities. The average church in America allocates about 5 percent of its budget for evangelism, but approximately 30 percent for buildings and maintenance. Another study reported that we are spending about $3 billion per year on the construction of new buildings.[2]

Whether we spend the money on buildings or evangelism, however, we are not seeing much progress in terms of expanding the community of believers. As reported earlier, there has been no growth in the percentage of adults who are born-again Christians. Perhaps it is not surprising, then, to report that our studies of the Protestant churches that are growing the fastest are expanding primarily by incorporating people from other, declining churches. This is growth by transfer, rather than by conversion. Thus, while many churches across the nation receive attention for their explosive growth, relatively few of those churches are attracting adults who are newcomers to the faith. Most frequently, they are simply enlisting individuals

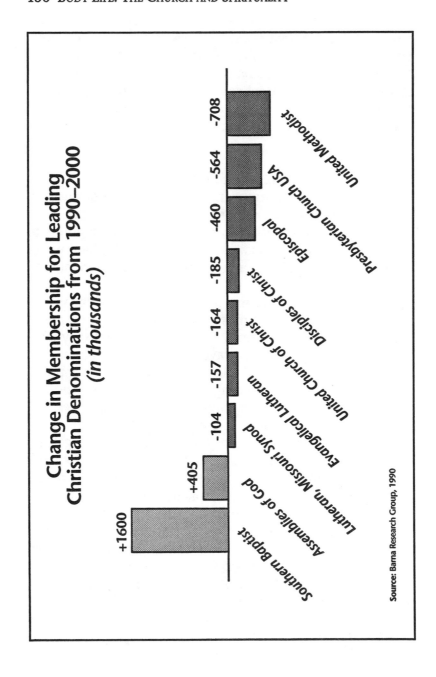

Change in Membership for Leading
Christian Denominations from 1990–2000
(in thousands)

+1600 Southern Baptist
+405 Assemblies of God
-104 Lutheran, Missouri Synod
-157 Evangelical Lutheran
-164 United Church of Christ
-185 Disciples of Christ
-460 Episcopal
-564 Presbyterian Church USA
-708 United Methodist

Source: Barna Research Group, 1990

who have left their existing church home to be part of the "happening" church. This is such a common behavior that an estimated 90 million adults in America have been "church shopping."[3]

Although the "megachurches" and "super churches" bask in the media spotlight, the reality is that most churches in America have fewer than 100 people in attendance on any single day of worship. The constant planting of new churches in communities across the nation is making it ever more difficult for churches to maintain a sizable and stable base of committed members.

Why Conversions Are Down

Churches do not grow by conversion for a number of reasons. Perhaps the most important of those is that regular participants in church activities do not invite their unchurched friends and neighbors to attend with them. One nationwide study conducted by Barna Research found that on any Sunday morning, one out of four unchurched people would willingly attend a church service if a friend would invite them to do so. That represents some 15-20 million adults each Sunday who could have been involved in a worship or spiritual learning experience if the Body of Christ had taken the responsibility for evangelism more seriously.

But the problems go even deeper. The image of the local church has taken a beating in recent years. Millions of Americans have turned their back on Christian churches because they believe it is hypocritical for churches to preach love, but exhibit rancor and division regarding denominational lines, theological distinctives or ethnic differences. Skeptics that we are, Americans are not about to patronize an institution which appears incapable of living what it preaches.

Confidence in the Church as a social institution is declining steadily. For many years, the Church stood as the most

Is the Church Today Relevant?
(Unchurched people respond)

 **YES** _38%_

 **NO** _62%_

Source: Barna Research Group

revered social institution. Today, it ranks third or fourth on the list. In fact, a growing percentage of adults believe that the Church at large is losing its influence upon society. This is important because we know that Americans—especially Boomers—do not want to associate with a "loser," whether it is a person or an organization.

Concern about churches does not end there. Only four out of ten adults say that the Church is relevant for today's world. Just one out of three Americans believe that the church is tolerant of people with different ideas. Significantly, notice that they believe the church rejects not just the different ideas, but the *people* who hold those ideas. Indeed, only a small proportion of adults say they would turn to the church for help in a time of personal crisis.

People's experiences at church are not especially positive, either. Substantial numbers of people do not describe their church experiences as inspiring, fulfilling, exciting or satisfying.

The State of Our Leadership

The clergy are not on solid footing these days. They are suffering from divorce at a rate that is rising even faster than among the general population. Alcoholism is an increasingly common problem among clergy. Studies of occupational groups suggest that pastors are among the most frustrated of all professional groups. This may account for the growing rate of turnover

---

Creating more churches will not solve the problem. This is like trying to make people read more by publishing more books.

---

within the pastorate, high burnout rates and shorter tenures among people in pastoral positions.

Research also shows that pastors are especially concerned about the health of the Christian Body in America. Just one out of three believe that the Church is having a positive impact on souls and society. Two-thirds say that the superficiality of people's faith is a very serious problem.

The most pervasive ministry frustration expressed by pastors is that they feel they bear the burden of ministry alone. Relatively few pastors feel as if they are part of a team of people working together to enhance the spiritual and social condition of the congregation and the world.

Changes are afoot within the clergy, too. A study conducted by the National Council of Churches found that the number of women who are clergy doubled between 1977-1986. While almost six out of ten female clergy can be found within just five denominations—Assemblies of God, Salvation Army, United Methodist, United Church of Christ and Presbyterian Church (USA)—the growing numbers of full-time women ministers has been yet another source of division between groups.

AMERICA, 2000

The '90s will be a decade in which the Christian Church becomes more aggressive in its attempts to bring adults back to Christ. The real question, however, is not the *will* of the church, but the *way* in which it will seek to persuade people to give it another chance.

Many denominations have targeted this decade as one for aggressive church planting. If existing plans are carried out, we can expect the number of Protestant churches in America to swell by another 75,000 congregations. During the decade, however, some 25,000 congregations will fade from existence. The net gain, then, should be about 50,000 churches by the turn of the century. In other words, expect at least 375,000 Protestant churches serving our country, dropping the number of adults per church to about 520.

Creating more churches, though, will not solve the problem. This is like trying to make people read more by publishing more books. The issue is not availability but perceived quality and relevance. It is likely that people will be even less aware of the churches in their community than they are today, despite some active marketing campaigns by various denominations and churches.

Further, we expect to see an increasing imbalance in the size of churches. The distribution of churches according to the number of people in attendance on an average weekend will show an even broader gap: there will be more megachurches (those with 2,000 or more regular attenders) and more minichurches (those with 75 or fewer people in regular attendance), with proportionally fewer congregations in between.

On the other hand, groups outside evangelical and mainline Christianity will continue to expand rapidly. The Mormon church will reach 10 million members by 2000, largely due to their emphasis on relationships between members. Eastern faiths, especially Buddhism and Islam, will more than double in the number of adherents. The New Age religions will prosper, although many of the groups that will be prolific by 2000 are not yet in existence.

Mixing and Matching

In general, America's religious faith in 2000 will be a combination of existing faiths. Known as syncretism, this approach to spirituality was quite common in Old Testament times (and earned the stern rebuke of the prophets). Americans, never quite satisfied with their options, and rarely pleased with old traditions and old rules, will create their own religions. They will mix and match the best of each faith to which they are exposed and emerge with a synthetic faith.

It will be fascinating to watch people develop these new religious philosophies. In all likelihood, they will seek a blend of elements that will give them a sense of control over life, personal comfort and acceptance and a laissez-faire life-style philosophy. It is likely that from Christianity they will borrow Jesus' philosophy of love and acceptance. From Eastern religions they will borrow ideas related to each person being his or her own god, the center of the universe, capable of creating and resolving issues through his or her own power and intelligence. From Mormonism they will extract the emphasis upon relationships and family, toward establishing a greater sense of community.

This grab bag approach to religion is, to some extent, what a few of the more progressive new age groups are already doing today. This process will expand so that we will have new religions developed in the next decade, to offer a more personal, less institutional reality than that which much of traditional Christianity has offered.

It is also likely that the ecumenical movement, stalled during the past couple of decades, will again move forward. As Christian groups become scared about the changes happening around them, and more denominations focus upon the potential of numbers rather than the power of theological differentiation, more bridges will be built across denominational lines. This will be a positive step toward causing Americans to see Christianity as a cohesive body.

The proportion of people who become formal members of a church will decline to less than 50 percent of the adult population. Adherence to a Protestant church will drop from the current 45 percent to about 38 percent. Church attendance on Sunday mornings will decrease to about 35 percent of the population on any given weekend. This figure would drop lower if it were not for the growing body of congregations that will change the long-standing pattern and offer worship services on Saturdays, and on Sunday afternoons, in addition to (or, occasionally, instead of) the traditional Sunday morning time.

Multiple "Church Homes"

One of the trends that church leaders will find distressing is the redefinition of the concept of a church home. Traditionally, individuals have evaluated the churches in their area and chosen a single local church to be their religious center. In the coming decade, however, increasing numbers of people will instead select between two and five local churches and consider those to be their *group* of home churches. On any given weekend, they will determine which church to attend according to their own most keenly-felt needs, and the programs each of their favored churches has to offer. Their financial support will be splintered among each of those churches, and the aggregate amounts given are likely to be less than average since they will have decreased loyalty and a softer commitment to any single church. Today, approximately 10 percent of adults follow this multiple church home pattern. By 2000, as much as

---

The denominations that will make the greatest headway in the '90s will not be the mainline churches, but those which are smaller and willing to take greater risks.

---

one-quarter of all adults involved with the Christian church may be involved in this approach.

Churches That Grow
The '90s will see churches become more aggressive in marketing and advertising In the early portion of the decade, telemarketing will be tried by thousands of churches. However, prospecting for new attenders will be done most commonly through direct mail advertising. Radio will become a more popular means of catching people's attention, since stations provide an opportunity to target a specific population niche more precisely than ever before. Newspaper advertising may also increase in use.

The denominations that will make the greatest headway in the '90s will not be the mainline churches, but those which are smaller and willing to take greater risks. Because they have less organizational inertia with which to contend, communicate a greater sense of purpose and urgency and are more focused on congregational growth, they will respond more quickly and more decisively than larger, more traditional denominations. Groups such as the Presbyterian Church in America and the Evangelical Free Church will grow most quickly.

Some observers have worried that as Boomers become a larger part of the Body, revenue for ministry will decline. The evidence suggests that this is an unfounded fear. What *is* true is that to motivate Boomers to part with their money, the church will no longer be able to sit back, request money and expect donations to roll in simply because it is the church. Boomers are searching for meaningful causes that use funds wisely and provide a tangible sense of impact. During the '90s, the Church will face stiffer competition for contributions, as the activist tendencies of Boomers cause them to give more consistently and more generously to nonreligious organizations. Local churches that provide compelling reasons for giving, that offer Boomers tangible personal benefits from giving, and that illustrate the impact of the donated funds will have the greatest success at fund-raising.

The odds are strong that people's perceptions of the Christian Church will not become more favorable. With the legal profession targeting churches as an industry very vulnerable to legal harassment and law suits; with the federal government encroaching upon the freedoms currently enjoyed by churches; and with nonprofit organizations rallying the population in response to a variety of environmental and sociopolitical agendas, the Church will lose its present standing as a moral and ethical leader, and as a stable moral foundation within the community. Unless substantial changes are made regarding the nature of religious practice within the Church, and by congregational members in their daily lives, nonbelievers will have little reason to alter their beliefs that the church is irrelevant, unexciting, of little help and having a decreasing influence on the course of our culture.

Changes in Church Leadership

Meanwhile, expect the number of women in the clergy to nearly double again during this decade. The men who enter the clergy will be older than any previous new crop of clergy, as more and more men leave their careers and pursue a ministry through the church. After a decade of catching up to the behavioral patterns of the people they serve, clergy will have crisis conditions—divorce, alcoholism, drug abuse—at rates that approximate those of the population at large.

The rate of constructing new buildings for churches is likely to peak in the early '90s, then decline. Newly constructed church buildings will reflect greater sensitivity to the audience being attracted and will include flexible designs (movable walls, ramps). Technology will be built in to the new buildings (VCRs, sound systems, automatic environmental controls in each meeting room), making it easier for church leaders to communicate with people in a more sophisticated and appealing manner.

✝ CHALLENGES AND OPPORTUNITIES FOR THE CHURCH

During the '90s, the Church must assume the same attitude as the environmental movement: it's time to get back to the basics. Our research has shown that people who regularly attend churches, as well as those who are investigating the value of Christianity, have a tremendous lack of understanding of the basic tenets of the faith. One particular study among Baby Boomers who are lay leaders indicated that such basic realities as worship are foreign concepts. Pastors and lay leaders often assume that every American understands the basic truths about God, Jesus, the Holy Spirit, salvation and damnation, sin and the like. Unfortunately, such assumptions are unfounded.

Rebuild the Foundations

This will be a decade in which we must refocus our energies upon restoring our foundation. People who ascribe to or who evaluate Christianity cannot automatically be assumed to be building on a solid foundation of truth. Being American no longer means to have a general comprehension of the belief structure of the Christian faith. More likely than not, the average adult who is either visiting a church or who is a relatively new or uninvolved member lacks knowledge of the fundamentals of Christianity.

These are the people who will be most susceptible to syncretism, even if they attend our churches and participate in our activities. We cannot afford to assume that we will influence their way of thinking by their mere presence in our buildings. There is just as good a chance that their beliefs may influence the perceptions of the individuals who have been most dedicated to Christianity—unless we can clearly delineate what Christianity is and is not, and why these distinctions are important.

Speak to Felt Needs

If we expect the Christian Church to attract more people, we will have to become more sensitive to their felt needs. The competition of the local church is not other churches down the street. It is television, sleeping in on Sunday, the weekend special at Bloomingdale's, games and picnics in the park and so forth. As people's lives become more tense, their time more valuable, and their skepticism about the influence and benefits of the church more confirmed, attracting people will be more difficult.

The best way to get the unchurched or nonbelievers to consider the Church valid and worthwhile will be by making ourselves relevant to their lives. How do we do that? By understanding their most pressing felt needs and responding directly to those needs. We can do this through the style of preaching;

the types of seminars and events sponsored by the Church; the ways in which we ask for and use people's money; and the ways in which the active participants in the Church interact with visitors.

Sensitivity to the needs and experiences of people is necessary if the local church is to broaden its appeal. Granted, there is no room for compromise in the message of the gospel. Once

---

If the church were to take the time and make the effort to identify their potential leaders' gifts, and permit them to use those gifts for ministry, there would be less volunteer burnout.

---

we compromise our basic beliefs, we cease to be the Church of Christ, and we take on the character of the New Age and syncretistic churches which are the tools of the Enemy. However, if we understand the thinking and needs of our target audience well enough, we can communicate with them in ways which are more meaningful to them. We can develop practices which do not undermine the truth of our beliefs, but which make those beliefs more real and tangible to the target population. In doing so, we must be more aware of how we are perceived, the impact of our words and practices, and the opportunities we have to provide substance and truth in creative and uncompromising ways.

Adults will seek tangible spirituality. It is not enough for us to talk about love. We must have a constant flow of activities in which we demonstrate that love (e.g., work with the homeless, children's literacy programs, blood drives). If we want people to give their money for ministry, we'll have to let them see and touch the products of their giving. Using video will be more important in this process (e.g., footage of missionary work in progress, interviews with people whose lives have been changed by the church's community ministry, etc.). To overwhelm people's doubts about the practicality of Christianity, we must demonstrate in real ways that what we believe can be lived and can make a difference in our world.

Hope—for Those Who Do Their Homework

All is not hopeless for the local church. Despite the uphill struggle facing most churches, realize that thousands of churches will grow in the number of participants they win over during the '90s. Why? Because they will do their homework. Those churches will understand the heartbeat of the community and gear ministry to meeting people where they are. Programs, staff appointments, budgets, communications—everything these churches do will be aimed at addressing the felt needs of the target audience.

Leadership will be a key component if the church is going to progress. Churches that grow in the '90s will be those that have a strong but compassionate leadership team. They will be churches that are focused upon God's vision of ministry for them, and pursue it with passion and excitement. Churches that are doing "business as usual" will fail to capture the attention and stimulate the interest of the average American adult.[4]

Involving Volunteers

For more churches to grow, both in numbers and in spiritual depth, a major overhaul of our approach to lay leadership must also transpire. Often, pastors complain that there are not enough people willing to be leaders in the church. In actuality, our research has shown that there are more than enough people capable and willing to serve in leadership roles. However, people will refuse to accept the burden of responsibility alone. They must be involved in team ministry, partnering with the clergy and other leaders to make ministry happen. Further, we must be more sensitive to volunteer burnout, placing a limit on how long we expect people to serve in any type of leadership capacity, and allowing them to reenlist if they so desire.

In addition, the ways in which we prepare people for involvement in ministry must be more hands-on. Today, most leadership training programs are carried out via lecture: we tell people *about* leadership, rather than nurture them in the *practice* of leadership. The success stories regarding lay leadership development are emerging from churches where leadership training is conducted through experience rather than talk.

As people's schedules become increasingly fragmented, and as they are faced with other options for volunteering, churches must be more competitive. One major step forward would be the revision of how we incorporate volunteers into church activity. Typically, churches take volunteers and place them into immediate service, attempting to fill the most pressing need of the moment. Their spiritual gifts and ministry calling frequently are not taken into consideration. The result is a frustrated individual, one whose true gifts may go unused, and who experiences aggravation over being asked to do tasks that are outside the realm of their ability. If the church were to take the time and make the effort to identify their potential leaders' gifts, and permit them to use those gifts for ministry, there would be less volunteer burnout and frustration, and a more productive lay ministry.

The church must initiate a revolution in its thinking about the laity. No longer can we afford to wait for visitors to walk in the back door, and hope they will find enough to their liking that they will come back again. The congregation must be trained to see itself as the marketing agents of the church, each person being responsible for spreading the gospel and for inviting people to come to church. More than ever, the personal touch will be effective in the '90s, as individuals desperately search for ways of feeling connected and means of building relationships. Since Christianity is about building up people, not programs or philosophies, this decade will be an important time for the Church to prepare its people to become local missionaries on behalf of Christ and the local Body.

Redefining Success

As our culture and social environment change, we must also consider the opportunity to redefine how we determine the success of a church. Typically, we do so by counting. We count the number of people who attend on Sundays. We count how many people are in Sunday School classes. We count the number of members in the church. We count how many dollars have been contributed for ministry and maintenance. We emphasize quantity toward determining the success of a church.

Perhaps the '90s will enable us to examine quality, rather than quantity, as a better indicator of success and church growth. If the experience of many of today's growing churches is any indication, the best means to gaining quantity is *through* quality: Americans are irresistibly drawn to those organizations that ooze quality. Given our shifting values, and the peaking interest in excellence and high standards, churches which evoke a sense of quality will be more attractive than those that simply continue to perform their usual routine, oblivious to standards.

Another area in which we must exhibit greater sensitivity is in how we support the clergy. Relatively few congregations do much to recognize the difficulties faced by the clergy, and to support them more extensively in their work. Most pastors and assistants need not only vacation time, but off-site study times; greater office and programs support; expressions of gratitude and appreciation; respect of their free time; and to be ministered to by the people during times of personal crisis (such as marital struggles, substance abuse). Rather than looking at clergy as people who are either perfect or failures, we must recognize them to be human beings who struggle with the same issues as the rest of us. How we support them through those struggles says as much about our grasp of Christianity as anything we do.

Notes
1. "Churches in America as of February 1990," (Arlington, TX: American Church Lists, February, 1990).
2. Constant Jacques, Jr., ed., *Yearbook of American and Canadian Churches, 1989* (New York: National Council of Churches, 1989), p. 280.
3. George Barna, *How to Find Your Church* (Minneapolis: World Wide Publications, 1989).
4. Barna, *Successful Churches: What They Have in Common* (Glendale, CA: Barna Research Group, 1990).

PART IV
CHANGES IN ATTITUDES AND PERCEPTIONS

We have to shed existing attitudes of piety and solemnness, in favor of attitudes of anticipation, joy and fulfillment. Christians must change the way we live nearly as much as nonbelievers must alter their perspectives.

9 ATTITUDES TOWARD SELF AND OTHERS

▶Americans want to be happy. They believe this requires being loved, having an impact on the world, finding security in life, living in comfort.

▶We *appear to* be satisfied with our lives; but inside there's an inner turbulence based on low self-esteem and a sense of purposelessness.

▶The '90s will bring heightened rancor related to rights of privacy. Racism will shift from disrespect toward blacks to animosity toward Hispanics.

▶The Church must help people develop a philosophy of life based on Christian principles, and create a new perspective on the purpose of life and more meaningful goals.

▶▶▶▶▶

ATTITUDES TOWARD OTHERS MAY BE THE SINGLE MOST IMPORTANT indicator of the character of a people. Since our most important behaviors and innovations are an outgrowth of our feelings and perceptions about people, we can gain acute insight into our culture by understanding those feelings.

 AMERICA, 1990

The average American adult perceives himself to be an intelligent, busy and capable individual. In general, we think of ourselves as religious, but not overbearing in our beliefs. We relate to the notion of being "conservative" more than "liberal," even though the chances are great that 20 years earlier we held liberal views on most sociopolitical issues, and that some of today's conservative views would have been viewed as liberal at that time. We would say we are decent, moral persons—more ethically sound, in fact, than we ever dreamed we might become. On the average, we feel that we are *not*—average, that is. Most of us feel that we are a cut above average. We do not admit to feeling stressed out, nor anxious about the future.

What We Want
What do we want out of life? Our surveys suggest that we have four primary goals, all related to "being happy." While most of us do not have a philosophy of life to guide our decision-making, we do react to situations and opportunities in light of these objectives.

How We Describe Ourselves

We think we are:

Busy (89%)
Conservative (72%)
Religious (63%)
Traditional (72%)
Curious (85%)
Successful (83%)
Well-educated (76%)
Patriotic (89%)
Well-informed (82%)
A leader (50%)
A moral leader (50%)

We do not think we are:

Scholarly (36%)
Stressed out (33%)
Workaholic (38%)
Liberal (42%)
Yuppie (9%)

Source: Barna Research Group, 1988-1990.

First, we want to be loved. We are driven to find acceptance from others, to belong to a group larger than what we, ourselves, represent. Significant relationships are critical to our sense of self-esteem, and of purpose.

Second, we want to make a difference in this world. For young adults this generally means engaging in overt demonstrations of kindness or societal sensitivity, designed to capture the attention of those in positions of authority, to prove to them that we are significant. As we age, the appeal of being acknowledged as an important somebody wears thin (especially for those who have succeeded in achieving such acclaim). Consequently, we focus more on helping others, thereby providing us with a sense of lasting impact. Often, however, this sense of impact supports our feelings of self-importance, underscoring our ability to control our environment and to direct the fortunes of others.

Third, we desire security. This might come in many forms, but the basic allure is the elimination of fear. Because our faith in life and self tends to be fragile, we harbor numerous fears about what might happen to us. Consequently, we strive to remove fear from our path.

Finally, we seek comfort. In contemporary America, this generally means the acquisition of wealth, and an abundance of leisure time. Comfort is both a sign of success, and the experience of pleasure.

How We Feel About What We Want

But how satisfied are we with our condition? While we are overtly pleased with ourselves and the life we lead, we have nagging doubts about our ability to ever find true and total happiness. We tend to see happiness as a fleeting emotion, rather than a life-style. We harbor disappointments that we have not achieved adequate levels of love, impact, security and comfort. Worse, despite our best efforts, we are not sure how we will ever reach those goals.

Psychologists tell us that these feelings of doubt, fear and insignificance are indicative of a nation of people suffering from low self-esteem. Although we continue to strive for material acquisition and relational harmony, most people nurse feelings of emptiness, as if they have failed to accomplish what they were designed to achieve.

During the past decade or so we initiated a transition related to our primary source of personal identity. Many years ago, our identity was a reflection of our family heritage. More recently, it became a reflection of our career. Increasingly, people are pointing to their life-style, with an emphasis upon their leisure activities, as the best indicator of who they are and what they stand and live for.

What We Say vs. What We Do

A careful evaluation of what we say, what we feel and what we do, however, indicates that we are a self-deceived nation. What we *say* we feel or believe is often an attempt to convince ourselves to accept that perspective. Our actions are often empty efforts at becoming something that, deep inside, we know we are not. We often give lip service to beliefs that are not in our heart.

Consider the following as just a few examples of the self-deception of the American people in 1990:

■ Although six out of every eight parents say that child care obligations should be shared equally by both parents, only one in eight parents actually do so.

■ Although nine out of ten parents expect their children to go to college, only half of those adults are saving money to help their offspring pay for that schooling.[1]

■ Americans typically identify their family life as their greatest source of happiness. Yet, we are increasingly likely to minimize the importance of keeping a marriage intact, to spend meaningful time with our children and to desire to engage in family activities during our free time.[2]

■ We extol the virtues of friendship, yet our own loyalties to other people are more fluid and unreliable than ever. Our friends are most likely to be the people who can be most useful to us at our stage in life. Because our lives are changing faster than ever, we find that our relationships are less enduring, too.

■ While four out of five Americans claim to be "Christian," that word has been made into a generic term referring to someone who is religious, believes in a universal force of some type or is simply a good person. We think of ourselves as "religious," even though half of us do not engage in consistent religious practices.

■ Some nine out of ten Americans say they are patriotic. However, when asked whether or not they would fight on the country's behalf if a war broke out, most adults indicate that they would engage in battle only if the war seriously threatened the geographic boundaries of the nation.

■ When it comes to ethics, we hold others to very high standards—standards we would typically fail to achieve in our own lives. Just look at the numbers of people who secretly cheat on their taxes, who sneak about to commit adultery, who use drugs but would not allow their children to do so, who break the speed limit when driving on the highway.

■ Ask the typical adult, and he or she will tell you that they work longer hours now than they did ten years ago. Research shows, however, that while we think we work more, we actually work less.[3]

Attitudes Toward Others

Our feelings toward other people have also become increasingly hardened. Racism and discrimination have accelerated in the past five years. Feelings about children have changed, such that many parents now look upon their youngsters as young adults, viable assistants whose value is increasingly determined by their ability to perform household functions such as shopping, home maintenance and training parents in high-tech applications. Even the value of life is relative these days, as interest in death sentences and life imprisonment for criminals has risen. The majority of Americans claim that while they would not have an abortion, the right to an abortion should not be denied to anyone.

In general, we are more likely to look upon other people as a means to an end. We are more likely to treat other people to be used for personal gain than was true two decades ago. When people threaten our ability to progress, we become irritated, frustrated or fearful, and are willing to have them removed from our environment. The concept of "community," connot-

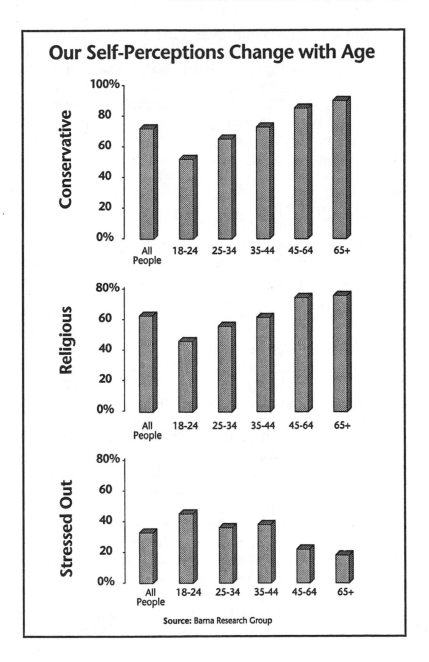

Our Self-Perceptions Change with Age

Source: Barna Research Group

ing a culture with pluralistic values and life-styles in which the people root for each other and strive to work out their differences toward achieving the common good, is anachronistic. In a nation founded on the principle of everyone working together for the benefit of the group, we have careened toward the opposite end of the spectrum, pursuing individual rights and personal gain, with little regard for the impact of those decisions and actions on others.

AMERICA, 2000

As our life-styles increasingly incorporate leisure activity as the centerpiece, we will have more time for reflection about who we are and how we relate to others. Will this time for reflection create a new understanding of self and community? Probably not. The bottom line is that Americans are likely to hold fast to their "take care of number one" mentality. As we strive to attain love, security, impact and comfort, we will devise unique philosophies which entreat others to accept us for what we are. As one advertising executive put it, the Baby Busters will be the first generation to care more about the products advertised than the people who advertised those products.

American adults will desire a favorable public image and a positive impact on others. However, we will be more likely to buy our way to a good image or to having a favorable impact on the lives of others than to change our basic attitudes and behaviors toward achieving the same ends. We will give our donations and volunteer our time more selectively, in ways designed to let others know just how compassionate and caring we are. While we will be less accepting of overt narcissism in others, we will continue to pursue the material trappings of success, simply being more low-key about it.

Criminal justice remedial programs, such as those seeking restitution rather than incarceration, will be politically appealing (due to cost savings) but emotionally repugnant to victims. People would rather have criminals locked up or killed than given the chance to rectify and reform.

My Way ... Your Way
The right to privacy, based on the deeply held conviction that this is a necessary aspect to individualism, will be a major issue

---

We will remain a society struggling with self-doubt and low self-esteem. As technological advances and the deterioration of social skills continue, Americans will feel increasingly isolated.

---

in the '90s. Many moral, ethical, religious and social issues will be defined as threats to our right to personal privacy.

Expect continued battles over abortion laws, as increasing numbers of people soothe their conscience by saying they personally would not have an abortion, but that it is the right of every woman to make that decision for herself.

Expect legal battles over new technologies that will provide protection and privacy for people. One such instrument would block incoming telephone calls from telephone numbers that have not been preprogrammed as acceptable by a homeowner. Lawsuits will be brought against companies for the invasion of privacy related to marketing efforts based on confidential financial information.

Racism and Self-Identity

Racism will persist. However, with increasing numbers of Hispanic immigrants, who will generally work as unskilled laborers and live in lower and working class immigrant neighborhoods, a major shift will occur. Hispanics will replace blacks as the ethnic group on the bottom rung of the social ladder. It is possible, though, that this upward movement for blacks may last but a decade, as Hispanics become more acclimated to America's life-styles and opportunities, and push for greater education and economic growth.

We will remain a society struggling with self-doubt and low self-esteem. As technological advances and the deterioration of social skills continue, Americans will feel increasingly isolated. Measures such as cohabitation will not fill the gap. Our dominant obstacle to emotional attachments will be our fear of being hurt and our unwillingness to sacrifice material comforts or leisure experiences in exchange for new relationships. Psychological counseling services will boom in the '90s, as people struggle with issues of self-worth, loneliness and control.

✝ CHALLENGES AND OPPORTUNITIES FOR THE CHURCH

The Christian Church is the only institution or body poised to provide meaningful answers to the emptiness and self-deception of our nation. The people of our country are severely damaged emotionally. We are a population of active, affluent people suffering from inner turmoil and strife that we try to hide even from ourselves. Even our times of joy and excitement are short-lived, and easily overwhelmed by the despair and fear that often follows such "up" times.

How can we respond to this hurting culture? It is imperative that we provide our people with insights into our condition, but without coming across as superior, or thinking we have it

Psychological Shifts for Christians to Pursue in American Culture

Today we seek to achieve:

COMFORT through the acquisition of material possessions, living a more prestigious life-style and enjoying increased leisure time.

SECURITY through acquisitions and actions designed to eliminate fears and maximize feelings of safety and the ability to survive turbulent times.

LOVE of self, concerned about making others accept us for who we are, as we are, toward feeding our desire to be important and to belong to something that makes us valuable.

IMPACT on the world, serving others so that we will be recognized as a good person and one whose life was meaningful, our passing will be the world's loss and people will fondly recall our ability to touch people's lives with money and creative intellect.

In the future, we should seek:

SERVICE to those around us, as a means of making their lives more meaningful, gaining the joy of helping others and the blessing of doing what God has called us to do.

FAITH in a God who has promised to provide for us, believing that He understands our needs and has our best interests at heart, and will respond on our behalf.

LOVE of others before ourselves, gaining self-love through our focus on others, and gaining acceptance from them because, as God did with us, we loved them first.

CONCERN about the plight of others, with the desire to see the world find peace and happiness through Christ; focusing on being as well as doing, more on sharing pain and love than blocking it from our consciousness.

all together. We must judge wrong behaviors, but not judge the people who commit those behaviors. The Church should be understanding and tolerant of the people, but neither accept nor legitimize sinful or pernicious actions.

Providing Better Options

In a culture which responds well to options and choices, we must develop means of providing people with attractive alternatives to their current attitudes and resulting actions. It is not enough to tell them "the Bible says." Americans need to have practical applications of principles, and to see those applications in practice. Modeling acceptable behavior will be critical.

How can we do this? First, we must help people to understand that we cannot gain a meaningful identity through the trappings of the world, but only through an understanding of our relationship with God, through Jesus Christ. Yet, our society has been virtually anesthetized to God-talk. Penetrating the consciousness of people will require practical demonstrations of faith in action; contemporary illustrations and descriptions of Jesus and His teaching; and making "church" less of the formal, sitting-in-the-pews on Sunday experience, and more of an in-the-world-serving-others adventure. We have to shed existing attitudes of piety and solemnness, in favor of attitudes of anticipation, joy and fulfillment. What we are saying implies that Christians must change the way we live and serve nearly as much as nonbelievers must alter their perspectives.

Revising Life Goals

Part of this process will be to help people develop a comprehensive philosophy of life, which will enable them to redefine their goals in light of a holistic perspective on life. This could lead to a revision of life's basic goals. Love of self could be replaced with a love of others. Striving for comfort could be replaced by an emphasis upon serving others. Faith could be substituted for the quest for security.

Unlike past attempts, though, we cannot hope to guide people to a better understanding of life, God, Christ and purpose by forcing our values and principles upon them. Americans want to discover ideas for themselves. We must allow people to arrive at these, or similar conclusions, through their efforts. Only then will they "own" those insights, and truly incorporate them into their life-styles.

The Church must stand fast against movements and organizations which seek to exalt personal rights over community interests. Prayer has been an underutilized weapon in the battle against excessive personal freedoms. But we must also provide relevant and well-reasoned teaching to our people about the Bible's perspectives on freedom and community, and on relationships with God, self and others.

Living Like We Love It!
Most of all, we must show nonbelievers what it looks like to be at peace with ourselves, and to truly love other people. The best means of creating an interest in Christ and the Christian way of life is to so thoroughly live and enjoy it that others will want to know how they, too, can have it.

Survey data show that most Americans believe that you cannot tell a born-again Christian from nonbelievers because there is no difference in the way they live. The only distinction, people say, is that Christians are more religious, more fanatical or more closed-minded. There is no widespread sense that the religious experience of Christians has changed the fabric of our thinking or the nature of our life-styles (other than requiring regular participation in church activities).

To convince a hardened and cynical world that we are not

just different, but better off for those differences, we must allow them to see how our struggles in life have been altered for the better as a result of our relationship with Christ.

Notes

1. Letter from *American Demographics* magazine, 1989.
2. Data from a Gallup survey reported in *Newsweek*, special issue, Winter/Spring, 1990, p. 18; data from Barna Research Group study conducted by Josh McDowell Ministries, 1987; data from Onmipoll, a tracking study by the Barna Research Group, 1988-90.
3. Statistics derived from studies conducted by Louis Harris & Associates and by the University of Maryland Survey Research Center, as reported in *Newsweek*, May 15, 1989, p. 57.

10 NEW STRESS ON INSTITUTIONS AND PROCESSES

CHAPTER HIGHLIGHTS:

▶Americans resist authority; we have a real problem with control.

▶Business is taking on more of the functions traditionally assumed by government.

▶We have grave concerns about the ethical behavior of businesses in America. Only 8 percent of us think business would not engage in common ethical abuses.

▶In the future, wars are more likely to be fought through computer maneuvering and economic sanctions than by bombs and battles.

▶People will redefine the role of companies in their lives, and will select their place of employment on the basis of factors other than salary.

▶For the local church to have a widespread impact on the community, it will have to engage in non-spiritual educational programs.

▶As America becomes more accustomed to filing lawsuits, be prepared for increasing numbers of legal challenges to the Church, clergy, staff—even lay leaders.

IN THE '60s, "THE SYSTEM" WAS THE INVISIBLE BUT OMNIPRESENT enemy. As the radicals of that era (today's Baby Boomers) have grown older and more conservative, they have redirected some of their ideology, but vestiges of their antiestablishment perspective can be found in their feelings about government, corporations and the social processes that make America tick. Their points of view have greatly influenced—and will continue to impact—our nation's attitude toward organizations.

 AMERICA, 1990

We may look mature and sophisticated, but we remain a nation that has a problem with authority. Millions of adults still bridle at being told what to do by an authority figure or institution. Control is the issue. Abdicating control over our lives is not something which we easily surrender. We respond best when we are involved in the decision-making process, when that process provides us with multiple choices and when the ultimate decision serves our own desires and best interests. Although we are not as overtly disrespectful of authority as the young adults of the late '60s were, to a great extent we have simply dressed up our antipathy toward those in power, and made our responses more socially acceptable.

Limited Loyalties

Today, the tension between government, business and the consumer has lessened. True to form, however, we have minimal

Americans Believe that Businesses Are Unethical

Do you believe that businesses...

47% would harm the environment

38% would endanger public health

37% would sell unsafe products

44% would knowingly sell inferior products

62% would deliberately charge inflated prices to make a profit

42% would risk employee health and safety

25% would do all of the above

8% would do none of the above

Source: Harris Poll, reported in *Business Week, 5/29/89, page 29.*

loyalty to any political representative, company, product brand or store. We are not about to make any standing commitments to institutions. We feel that an institution must prove itself worthy of our respect or patronage each time we interact with it.

Part of our refusal to commit ourselves to existing institutions or corporations is the rapid change taking place within many industries. The stability that used to breed confidence in an industry or organization can no longer be assumed. For instance, people are less loyal to banks today, given the recent discovery that financial institutions may go under without warning, sucking up the assets of their patrons without any viable recourse or protection. Or, with leveraged buy outs and hostile takeovers and makeovers, even a company that has a long-respected name and image may no longer have the same corporate culture, personality or style.

This limited loyalty means that we are willing to restructure the traditional lines of responsibility and authority between government, business and individuals. Our willingness to give corporate America a shot at providing services historically provided by the government is especially evident in the areas of education, transportation and communications.

Businesses are increasingly involved in launching private schools and in developing adult training programs. Private companies are now building toll roads (a pilot project is now underway in Virginia, with others to follow in California and elsewhere). The concept was designed to remove the burden of road construction and maintenance from the state, awarding it to an aggressive, lean corporation, which could make a profit, provide superior service, and create potential tax benefits for the public. Thousands of companies now rent mail boxes to people for mail delivery at places other than the post office. Several dozen other companies are seeking ways to replace the U.S. Postal Service as the dominant mail carrier. These are just a few examples of our growing desire to convert government operations into free enterprise system opportunities.

Corporate Cautiousness

Yet, while we endorse the private provision of goods and services to the population, we are cautious about corporate America, too. According to research conducted by Lou Harris, most Americans believe that businesses engage in unethical practices as standard behavior. Millions of people believe that businesses would knowingly harm the environment, endanger public

---

Millions believe that businesses would knowingly harm the environment, endanger public health in pursuit of corporate profits, sell products known to be unsafe, consciously market products of inferior quality and risk employee health and safety.

---

health in the pursuit of corporate profits, sell products known to be unsafe, consciously market products of inferior quality and risk employee health and safety. In fact, Harris concluded that only 8 percent of the adult population believed that corporations would not engage in any of these practices.[1]

Americans are increasingly willing to protest the actions of both government and business. Campaigns connected to social issues—abortion, AIDS discrimination, racial injustice, gay rights, environmental abuse, nuclear power, pornography, drug abuse, drunk driving—routinely win widespread support and involvement in communities across the land.

While the hippies of the '60s made their feelings known

through marches, sit-ins and other public protests, the maturing Boomers have learned to make their views known by working through the political process (e.g., referenda on state and local ballots), the media and very deliberate spending patterns. Concerted efforts (through product boycotting and viewer letters to network officials) to cause television networks to drop violent or sexually promiscuous programming have had some positive impacts. Stockholder protests and stock dumping have pushed major corporations to divest their holdings in nations which have policies of racial discrimination. Grassroots campaigns aimed at lobbying lawmakers have resulted in stiffer state laws dealing with drivers who are drunk or on drugs. These changes resulted from sophisticated campaigns that avoided marches in the streets and public name calling.

Governmental Guardedness
Despite our decision to coexist with a bloated government, we still refuse to hand over control to it. Americans continue to resist attempts at further government regulation, except when private efforts to provide specific services or programs have failed. The Reagan Revolution of the '80s, despite its faults, did manage to deregulate a number of industries, such as the airlines and cable television. Repeated attempts at regulating new industries and socializing others (such as health care) are fought tooth and nail.

AMERICA, 2000

The '90s will stem the steady decline in the public's confidence in institutions. While we will remain cautious and skeptical, greater efforts by institutions at enhancing the quality of life in the community, plus the fact that people from the Boomer

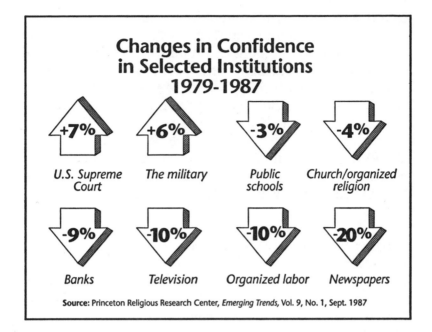

Changes in Confidence in Selected Institutions 1979-1987

+7% — U.S. Supreme Court

+6% — The military

-3% — Public schools

-4% — Church/organized religion

-9% — Banks

-10% — Television

-10% — Organized labor

-20% — Newspapers

Source: Princeton Religious Research Center, *Emerging Trends,* Vol. 9, No. 1, Sept. 1987

generation will control the most influential institutions, will disarm some of our mistrust. Although we will retain reservations about some institutions (most notably our public schools and the police), we will assume a more upbeat perspective about our key social organizations.

Power Games

However, we will continue to have a sense of uneasiness about government and national security. The uneasiness will arise from the feeling that we are truly pawns in a larger, more intense game. As technology advances, wars will no longer be fought on a battlefield with conventional weapons. Computers will control economic sanctions and trade decisions, and determine strategic positioning through simulation and gaming techniques. This will represent another tangible element of control and comprehension removed from our grasp, causing us to feel both intimidated and powerless.

Some of the organizations which formerly held considerable power will fade from sight. The most prolific will be labor unions, many of which will become virtually dormant by 2000. A few, such as those operating in Hollywood, will remain intact. However, with a shrinking working class, with ethnic groups comprising the low-skilled labor force and with unions unable to provide sufficient bargaining strength and unique benefits for members, interest in paying dues and remaining loyal to these groups will plummet.

Business: Pluses and Minuses
Americans will have a love-hate relationship with business. On the positive side, people will rethink their feelings toward businesses, perceiving them to be an extension of family. Corporations and small companies will assume ever greater roles in the areas of health care, child care, elder care and employee education. People will also appreciate the investment by businesses in community and cultural development. In fact, much of the mass media advertising of 2000 will be geared to portraying the worthy social character of corporate America, designed to build people's confidence in those organizations. (The hard sell will come through more targeted media, such as direct mail.) Advertising will show people the humane side of the organization.

In the '90s, we will have increasing numbers of small businesses, many run by husband-wife teams (called co-preneurs). These small operations, many of which will encompass small staffs of employees, will also cause people to view the business world as more sensitive and understanding.

On the negative side, however, will be people's frustration with the inability of companies to provide satisfactory career path. The abundance of experienced, educated Boomers will clog the middle management ranks, choking the entry way to the executive level. Further, the widespread introduction of artificial intelligence into the marketplace will cause many people to lose their positions to more cost-efficient technological replacements. Thus, the corporation will be viewed as a heartless, unappreciative entity that cannot be trusted.

Other individuals will harbor resentment toward corporations for their environmental abuses. With protection and recovery of the environment one of the leading causes of the '90s, the media will spend immense amounts of time focusing on organizations whose performance leaves something to be desired from an environmental standpoint.

The compensation package will no longer be the most critical element in a potential employee's decision about signing on with a company. Other factors, such as the company's image, its policies for helping employees with nontaxable benefits (e.g., child care) and flexible work schedules, as well as the fulfillment gained from the work itself, will become dominant.

Changing Ways of Change

Expect to see (or participate in) even more protests against ethical slippage by business and government. Whereas one out of three adults had participated in some protest in 1990, more than half of all adults will have done so by 2000. Interestingly, although we will truly be living in a global economy by then, the focus of our activism will be upon what happens to our households and our communities. Because we will be increasingly overwhelmed by the complexity of the world system, we will try to manage life by reducing our dilemmas and crises to a series of bite-size pieces. Having made our universe of problems more approachable, we will then chip away until we see progress. We will attack government and corporations relative to those actions which hinder our quality of life in the home or in our locale.

We can also expect the nature of our interactions with institutions to become more sophisticated and complicated. Advances in database management will better arm government and business to track our behavior and benefit from such knowledge. We will also find America increasingly litigious. Attorneys will be ever-present, partially the result of our law schools producing an overabundant supply of lawyers. Anx-

---

Government will become more regulation-minded. Some industries that were deregulated in the '80s will be reregulated in the '90s.

---

ious to make their careers, we will witness a court system that is hopelessly choked with waiting cases; a Supreme Court that is backlogged with a prolific caseload of constitutional challenges; and an edgy and aggressive spirit within the legal profession. While the prevailing "taking care of number one" philosophy will be the foundation of millions of unnecessary lawsuits, lawyers, as a profession, will most likely suffer a tarnished image as a result of their aggressive hostility.

Government, meanwhile, will become more regulation-minded. Expect some of the industries that were deregulated in the '80s to be reregulated in the '90s. Also anticipate regulation of religious organizations (regarding fund-raising practices, income reporting and professional licensing), and more stringent monitoring and enforcement related to environmental abuses.

By 2000, voting participation statistics will reach higher levels than have been achieved for several decades. Boomers will vote in record numbers, as a means of protection, self-expression, and control. Referenda will be more common in most states by 2000, as Boomers seek to take control over more of the public decision-making apparatus in order to make laws and policies that will impact their lives more favorably.

✝ CHALLENGES AND OPPORTUNITIES FOR THE CHURCH

The Church can become a powerful influence in America if it can assume a more significant role in the realm of education. This does not mean that we turn our backs on our spiritual calling; to the contrary, it is because of that calling that we have to become positioned as an educational institution.

Why? The opportunities we will face in reaching people whose minds are closed to the gospel will be educational in nature. People will demonstrate increasing interest and participation in the political process. There will be a need for education about the issues. The Church can play a vital role in that process. People will be searching for meaning and purpose in life. The Church can be an agent of information and insight. People will be more active in social causes, and require additional knowledge about opportunities for service. The Church is already in a position to guide people into meaningful roles for community service.

Educational vs. Authoritative

We also have to be careful as to how we are perceived by the masses. If we continue to pose as an institution whose position is based on authority (i.e., we ought to be respected and accepted because we have legitimate authority in the national social structure), we will merely threaten people and chase them off. If, however, we position the Church as an educator, or perhaps as a social institution whose primary role is to facilitate relationships between like-minded individuals, then we are meeting a felt need without threatening people. If what we have to offer is viewed as attractive and venerable, we become viable. If we maintain the traditional Church posture—i.e., we are the morality police, or we are the judge and the jury of mankind —we will be dismissed as an outdated institution.

Remember, too, that we are in a society in which institutional loyalty has reached a low point. During the '90s, people will investigate all types of religious groups, regardless of their personal religious heritage. Even those who find something attractive within the Church will make short-term commitments, at best. But realize, too, that those commitments are renewable, at the option of the individual.

We can gain people's confidence not by raving about pure spiritual truths, but about truth as it relates to people's daily struggles. If we are sensitive to feelings of powerlessness and insignificance, we can address those feelings with biblical principles, and do so without sounding pious and self-righteous. We can introduce people to concepts of the real game—the spiritual war taking place around us—once we have established their confidence and trust. But we must meet people where they are at first, before we explore deeper truths on other dimensions.

Confrontations to Confront

Personally, each of us in leadership positions must be prepared for legal encounters. Thousands of lawsuits, not only against clergy but also against staff and lay leaders, will be lodged in the '90s. Churches should make provisions in their budgets to carry sufficient liability insurance to protect the leaders, and may consider insuring (or otherwise protecting) lay leaders. Family and psychological counselors may be especially vulnerable during the '90s, as more people seek advice and counsel, but find the outcomes frustrating or unsatisfying. Local churches may wish to investigate the value of hiring a staff attorney to provide ongoing advice, to circumvent potential legal battles.

We can also prepare to band together to fight new drives to eliminate religious freedoms enjoyed by the local church. The attack will come from both government agencies (e.g., IRS) and nonreligious organizations (e.g., ACLU, NOW). Huge amounts of money will be spent on Capitol Hill lobbying legislators toward making churches accountable to the government. It is not too early to begin praying about this situation. Eventually, churches in the community might band together to prepare reasonable and persuasive responses to the likely lines of attack. Part of the group effort would be the development of strategies for communicating those responses to the community, and determining how to motivate people to direct the thoughts of their legislators on this issue.

In the days ahead, the Church would do well to recognize the growing cadre of co-preneurs in the congregation, and learn viable marketing techniques from those people. The ones who are successful could certainly inform church leaders about current and effective techniques, and adapt those for use by the Church.

Note
1. *Business Week*, May 29, 1989, p. 29.

PART V

WHO AND WHERE AND HOW WELL OFF WE'LL BE

America's population is growing primarily through immigration. By 2000, the native-born Caucasian population will experience zero population growth.

11 THE HEAD COUNT: POPULATION GROWTH AND DISTRIBUTION

CHAPTER HIGHLIGHTS:

▶The 1990 census will show that America has approximately 250 million people. That is 23 million more people than in 1980, representing a 10 percent increase.

▶The fastest-growing areas of the nation are states in the south and southwest. Although the national population will grow by 7 percent in the coming decade, one-fourth of our states will have fewer residents in 2000 than in 1990.

▶The church can achieve numerical growth and ministry impact by establishing ministries geared to minorities; by redefining what it means to be an urban church; and by following up on church members who have moved away. ▶▶▶▶▶

SIMPLY KNOWING HOW MANY PEOPLE LIVE IN AMERICA REVEALS LIT-tle about the future of the nation. However, by understanding more about the *changes* in the population—the rates of growth, what geographic areas are experiencing growth, population groups that are growing the fastest and the reasons for growth and decline—we can gain insight into what to expect in the way of social issues, resource needs and ministry opportunities.

 ## AMERICA, 1990

The 1990 census will show that America has approximately 250 million people. That is 23 million more people than in 1980, representing a 10 percent increase.

The Immigrant Nation
The bulk of this increase came from a new source: immigration. During the '80s, the native-born population experienced minimal growth (about 4 percent). Most of the nation's population growth can be attributed to the fact that the Asian population increased at twelve times the rate of the native-born population, and the Hispanic population increased at five times the native-born rate.

Immigration, then, has become a cornerstone of America's plans for expansion and prosperity. In 1990, America will accept more immigrants than all other nations of the world combined. Recognize, too, that these figures count only *legal* immigrants. Estimates of the number of illegal immigrants entering America each year range from 50,000 to 500,000.

As a consequence of our openness to immigration, America

has become the world's melting pot. We now have more Jews than Israel. We have more Irish than Ireland. There are more blacks in America than in any other nation of the world except Nigeria. Only Mexico and Spain have more Hispanic people than the United States.

The flood of immigrants has brought the black population to a major turning point. Blacks have traditionally been thought of as being on the bottom rungs of the economic ladder in America. However, significant strides in educational achievement by blacks, combined with the lack of education, literacy and job skills among many Hispanic immigrants, has pushed the black community higher in the economic and social status hierarchies of America. While we still have enormous proportions of blacks who are undereducated and live below the poverty level, the entry of the Hispanic population has changed the relative social status of the black community.

New Household Patterns
Other significant shifts underscore the startling transformation taking place in American society. The size of the average family (3.17 people) and of the average household (2.64 people) has hit new lows.[1] This is due to several converging factors. Marriage rates have continued to decline, reducing the possibility of childbearing. Among those people who do get married, fewer are having children. Even those couples that do have children are having fewer than at any prior time in our history. Fertility rates have dropped to the lowest level on record. And despite our esteemed medical facilities and practitioners, our infant survival rate is surprisingly poor: the United States ranks 20th in the world.[2]

Adding to the low birth rate is the continued prevalence of divorce, with more than half of all new marriages ending in divorce within 10 years. The statistics also show that married adults are waiting longer to have their first child. This results in one of two outcomes: older parents, or the couple dissolving their marriage before having any children at all.

Also, births out of wedlock are increasing substantially, having risen 32 percent since 1980. Of every fifteen children born today, one is born to unmarried parents. This is partially a result of the increased prevalence of cohabitation among adults.

Where We Live

America's population has continued to shift southward, departing from the northeast and north central states to the warmer climates of the south and southwestern states. This movement began in the '70s and has continued unabated for the past 20 years.

At the same time, most of the growth we have enjoyed has occurred within our cities. In 1950, barely half of the nation lived in an urban area. Today, more than three-quarters of all Americans (77 percent) reside in a city or suburb. The move to the cities has been strengthened by immigration, as most newcomers to America head for the largest cities. Each of the major immigrant ethnic groups have several cities where there are enclaves of people who speak their native language and maintain their native customs and culture.

Transience has become a way of life for Americans. Currently, one out of five households changes its address each year. More than eight out of ten relocate within the same state. In fact, most of those moves are either within a metropolitan area or to a nearby city.

 AMERICA, 2000

When the census takers count heads in April, 2000, it is expected that they will enumerate 268 million Americans, an increase of just 18 million people over the 1990 count. That

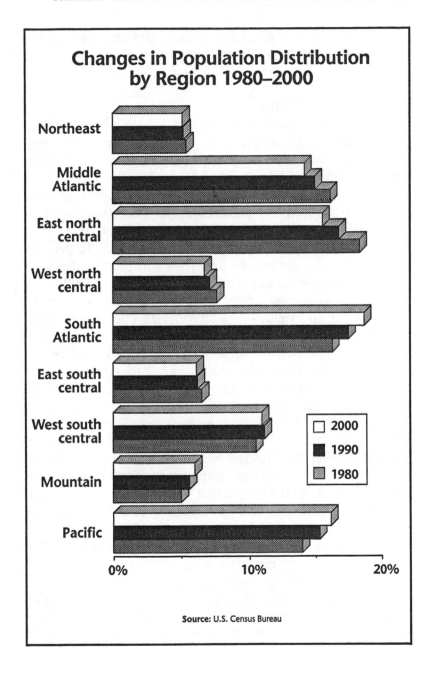

Changes in Population Distribution by Region 1980–2000

Northeast

Middle Atlantic

East north central

West north central

South Atlantic

East south central

West south central

Mountain

Pacific

☐ 2000
■ 1990
▨ 1980

0% 10% 20%

Source: U.S. Census Bureau

means that during the coming decade, the aggregate rate of population growth will slow to about 7 percent.

The Changing Hues

We can expect the native-born, Caucasian population to continue to experience a declining fertility rate, reaching zero population growth rate by 2000. Barring unforeseen changes in our immigration laws, blacks and immigrants will be responsible for all of the net increase in the population that takes place at the end of the decade. Both the Asian and Hispanic populations are likely to increase by 35-40 percent in this decade. The black population will increase by 15 percent. Overall, the proportion of minorities will increase from 23 percent of the population in 1990 to 26 percent in 2000.

The changing hue of America—a shift from white to brown, black and yellow—will support the continued expansion of the economy. Asians tend to be better educated and to have higher household incomes than the average white, native-born American. The Asians have proven their ability (and desire) to adopt American cultural habits and to thrive in the business environment.

With the transition of Hong Kong from a British colony to Chinese control in 1997, we can expect to see an influx of affluent families from Hong Kong occurring before the transition date. Asian immigration from other nations will also continue to escalate as the Pacific Rim becomes the world's dominant economic center, and as countries' economies become more global than national in their focus and activity.

Although Hispanics achieve lower levels of education than other population groups, they will be welcomed by service-oriented businesses throughout the '90s, as there will be a shortage of workers to fill low-skill, low wage jobs. The explosive population growth of Mexico and other Central American and South American nations will provide a steady stream

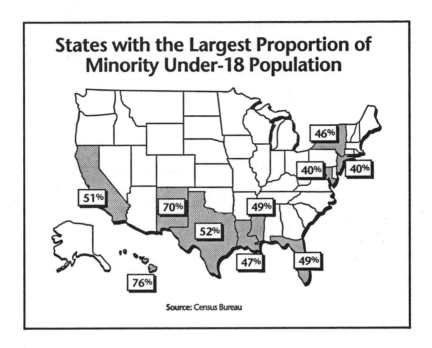

States with the Largest Proportion of Minority Under-18 Population

Source: Census Bureau

of Spanish-speaking people seeking admission to this country.

Despite continuing gains in overall academic achievement, blacks will continue to struggle with social and economic polarization. Increasing numbers of black Americans will either be living below the poverty level or among the affluent.

Another significant impact of accelerating immigration is on the youth population. Immigrant youths represent a higher proportion of the youth population than their parents represent in the American adult population. In 1990, 31 percent of all children under 18 were minorities. By 2000, that figure will grow to 34 percent. In certain cities (such as Los Angeles), ethnic minorities will actually be the majority population, as native-born whites decrease in proportion. The cultural impact of this minority presence on our school systems is, and will continue to be, of major importance.

Changing Population Centers

The move to the cities and to the warmer states will continue without interruption during the '90s. By 2000, four out of five Americans will live in a metropolitan area. Each of the 10 areas that will add the *most people* to their population totals will be in the southern half of the country: Los Angeles, Anaheim,

---

If you want to meet foreigners, stay in America —they're all coming here, either to live or visit.

Dallas, Atlanta, Oakland, Tampa, St. Petersburg, Phoenix, San Jose, Denver and Sacramento. In terms of the *percentage* growth, nine of the top ten metropolitan areas will be located in the southern portion of the U.S.—five in California, three in Florida, and one in Texas. (The lone non-southern urban center will be Atlantic City, NJ.)

One-fourth of the states (13) will actually have fewer people in the year 2000 than in 1990. Among the 37 states that will experience absolute growth in numbers of people, nine of those will add 15 percent or more to their 1990 population level. The fastest-growing states in the coming decade will be Arizona, New Mexico, Florida, Georgia, Alaska, Hawaii, New Hampshire and California.[3]

Transience is projected to continue at about the same pace as during the '80s (20 percent moving each year). Although the Boomer generation is aging and seeking to gain greater stability in life, the turmoil of divorces, the decreasing likelihood of

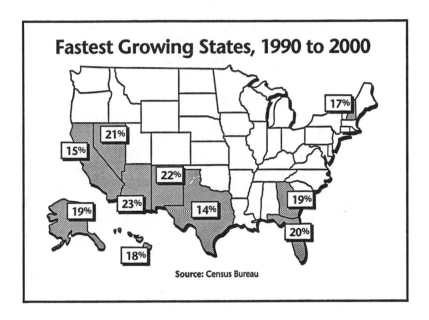

Fastest Growing States, 1990 to 2000

Source: Census Bureau

owning a home, and the constant search for a better, more ful-filling career and life-style will keep millions of Americans en route to a new home each year.

CHALLENGES AND OPPORTUNITIES FOR THE CHURCH

The Church in America has promulgated Christianity as a white man's faith for many decades. If the Church hopes to stem its current decline in numbers and influence, it must embrace minorities not only as equals, but as a key to future impact in ministry. Today, we look upon successful minority congregations as a novelty. In general, the Christian body commits little effort to paving the way for successful minority ministry.

The importance of attending to the spiritual life of immigrant groups is underscored by surveys which show that Asians and Hispanics are less likely than native-born whites and blacks to have accepted Christ as their Savior, or to have made any type of commitment to Jesus Christ.

"Over There" Is Over Here

How interesting that this opportunity is upon us at this moment in time. For the past five years, parachurch agencies geared to sending American missionaries overseas have been lamenting the fact that many nations around the world are closing their doors to our missionaries. Perhaps God is providing a partial solution to such inaccessibility by relocating the mission field within America! (As one observer put it, if you want to meet foreigners, stay in America—they're all coming here, either to live or visit.)

The health of the American Church will depend upon its ability to attract minorities to Jesus Christ, and to equip and activate them for ministry. We must establish new congregations offering worship services, music and prayer, educational programs, relational opportunities and social services in other languages, recognizing and celebrating different customs. Denominations must aggressively promote such activity. Seminaries must prepare minority representatives for leadership. The existing Church body must assist in the development of new minority-oriented churches and parachurch ministries if such a broadening of the Christian faith in this country is to happen.

The Church should also play a more aggressive role in serving the daily needs of minorities. There are substantial opportunities to assist immigrants in assimilating American culture and language. The Church could help ease the transition from old country to new homeland by understanding the customs and needs of these people, and addressing them with sensitivity. This may mean developing novel programs that provide housing location assistance; English language tutoring; literacy programs; financial planning and management assistance; and bilingual child care.

Where to Focus

As the turn of the century approaches and new churches are planted across the nation, the wisest strategy would be to locate those congregations in areas where the population is moving and growing. This means focusing upon the southern half of the nation. It means establishing strong urban ministries, not just providing a local presence in suburbs. The coming decade will provide ample opportunities for establishing new and vibrant churches within our cities, and addressing the peculiar needs of city dwellers.

Most churches would agree that they are partly responsible for the spiritual well-being of their own members. Yet, we have developed the "out of sight, out of mind" philosophy regarding transient people. Rather than continue to care for the spiritual development of people after they leave the community and are seeking to establish themselves in new surroundings, we write them off as a piece of history.

Local churches must retain responsibility for tracking the spiritual well-being of transients who move from the community. Research consistently shows that the greatest strength of the Church is its ability to enable people to develop meaningful relationships with others in the body. And the research also shows that people are most likely to find a church home when friends whom they know and trust incorporate them into the life of a church. As people continue to move from community to community, the Church should help departed members locate a new church home that will further their spiritual growth.

Notes
1. U. S. Census Bureau.
2. U. S. Centers for Disease Control.
3. "Population Growth and Shrinkage," *Adweek*, September 11, 1989, p. 42; U. S. Department of Commerce, Bureau of the Census.

12 REDEFINING "OLD": THE AGING OF AMERICA

CHAPTER HIGHLIGHTS:

▶Because the American population is older than it has ever been, we will lose our focus on youth. The median age, currently 33, will continue to rise; Baby Boomers will reach their 50s in 1996.

▶In response to aging, our environment will be redesigned to facilitate comfort and convenience; employers will institute new policies and programs to allow the elderly to continue working; and people will assume more positive attitudes about being old.

▶The church should put tremendous resources into youth ministry—while there are still millions of reachable children.

▶Ministries must refocus on the changing needs of the adult population to address the needs of older adults.

Since Columbus walked the shores of America, our nation has been geared to youth. The median age of Americans has always reflected the relative youth of the population, and adults have generally fueled this youth-orientation by lavishing devotion and attention upon their children. But as the pages of our history turn we are entering a new chapter, one in which the focus is rapidly shifting from the young to the old.

AMERICA, 1990

American culture has been dominated by the Baby Boom generation for nearly four decades—and they will continue to determine the heart of the American life-style and mind-set. Born between 1946-1964, the 76 million Boomers represent the largest generation in America's history—and one of the most radical in their determination to define life according to their own desires.

The Senior Surge
The Boomers are not the only story, though. Advances in health care, medicine, nutrition and leisure technology have helped increase the average life expectancy to 78 years. The median age of Americans is now in the mid-30s, and will pass 40 early in the next century.

Senior citizens represent one out of every eight Americans. With the dearth of children born between 1965-1978, there are now more senior citizens in this country than there are teenagers—a first in our history. As recently as 1960, we had twice as many 5- to 13-year-olds as we had people 65 or older.

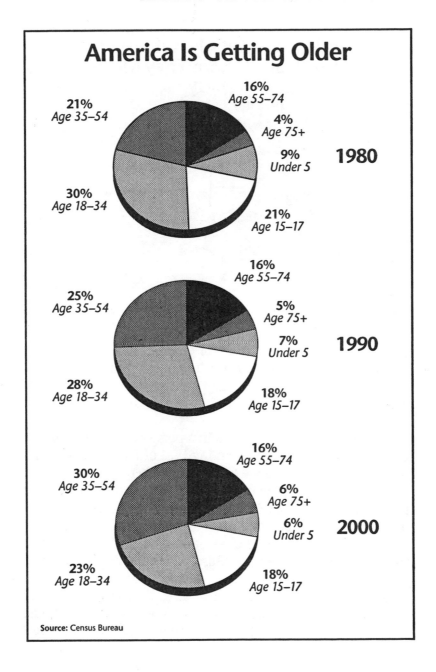

America Is Getting Older

16%
Age 55–74

21%
Age 35–54

4%
Age 75+

9%
Under 5

1980

30%
Age 18–34

21%
Age 15–17

16%
Age 55–74

25%
Age 35–54

5%
Age 75+

7%
Under 5

1990

28%
Age 18–34

18%
Age 15–17

16%
Age 55–74

30%
Age 35–54

6%
Age 75+

6%
Under 5

2000

23%
Age 18–34

18%
Age 15–17

Source: Census Bureau

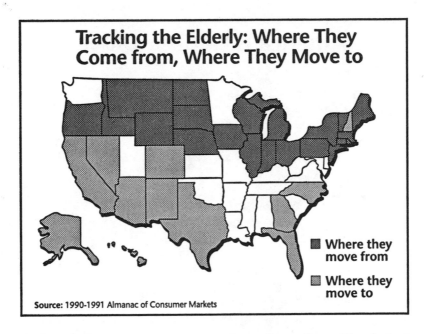

Tracking the Elderly: Where They Come from, Where They Move to

■ Where they move from
▨ Where they move to

Source: 1990-1991 Almanac of Consumer Markets

Today, those two segments are of equal numbers. The fastest growing age segment in America today, proportionally, is the 85 and older set. By 2010, they will be twice as numerous. Between 1980-1990, the number of people over the age of 100 more than tripled.[1]

One gerontologist helps us gain a perspective on the significance of America's aging by noting that of all the people who have ever lived past the age of 65, half of them are alive now.

Although the number of children is on the decline, and our senior population is exploding, the Boomers' children are having a dramatic impact on the nation. Not only have marketers seized the opportunity to develop and sell kids' products to this burgeoning market; the "Busters" are causing a transition in our national infrastructure.

During the late '70s and early '80s, thousands of school buildings and related facilities were sold or boarded up because the school-aged population plummeted after the Boomers moved through the system. Now, however, the children of the Boomers (also known as the Baby Boom Echo or Baby Boomlet) are creating the need for increased classroom space and more teachers. Growth in the elementary school population will peak in 1990, although that population will continue to grow at lower levels over the next six years.

AMERICA, 2000

The American population will be nearly evenly distributed between children, young adults, middle-aged adults and the elderly. The transition will have been completed from a youth-heavy society to one which is less imbalanced by age. We will also be a society that is more acutely aware of the differences in attitude and life-style associated directly with age, and intergenerational conflicts may intensify as each age segment vies for control.

The turn of the century will also bring two major shifts: the swelling of high school enrollments, and Baby Boomers coming face-to-face with the reality of becoming part of the "mature" market.

Enrollment in grades kindergarten through eight will escalate through 1996. In the mid-'90s, the focus of growth will shift to the high schools. During the last five years of the '90s, the enrollment in high schools will grow three times faster than that of elementary and junior high schools. Once again, there will be a substantial need for additional facilities and teachers to handle the Boomlet population.[2]

Aging and the Economy
The '90s will be an interesting time for the economy. Two-thirds of the adult population will be at what we consider the prime working age (25-54). But "prime working age" may be

redefined along the way. The Rand Corporation is projecting that the average life expectancy will jump to 90 by the turn of the decade, providing people with more years in which they can work without giving up a suitable number of retirement years.

By 2010, one out of four senior citizens will also have children living who will be senior citizens.

We are already seeing a revision of the notion of retirement. The average retirement age, now 60, will likely rise over the next decade, as more seniors decide not to leave the work force. Studies indicate that more and more elderly people, physically and mentally capable of continued work, desire employment—not primarily for the money, but because it provides them with control over their lives, a sense of fulfillment and the stimulation of challenge.

Corporations will respond to the desire of older adults to remain employed by introducing new policies and programs. Among the innovations we can expect are:

■ Retraining programs, in which older workers are given specialized education to update their skills, and make them more valuable to the company.

■ Sabbaticals, or extended periods of leave, during which the individual can pursue personal interests—leisure, education, health enhancement, etc. The leave of absence will be unpaid, but the person's job will be reserved for them until their return.

■ Phased retirements, allowing older adults to cut back on their work loads or hours, without cutting their job ties altogether.

■ Part-time employment, in positions providing lower pay, lower visibility, and lower stress, but greater flexibility in hours.[3]

Other Adjustments Due to Aging

While the 65-plus population may be more active and productive than has traditionally been the case, there will also be some new strains placed on the population as a result of aging. Elderly care will be one of the dominant issues of the '90s. By 2010, one out of four senior citizens will also have children living who will be senior citizens! To meet the coming demand for elderly housing, we would have to add more than 200 new nursing home beds per day on a daily basis through the year 2000. It is likely that nursing homes, elderly dormitories and retirement villages will be the focus of the construction industry in the next 20 years, as the elderly housing market will increase more than tenfold in revenues.

The influx of Boomers into the ranks of those eligible for Social Security and Medicare benefits will heighten the political debate about the solvency of those programs.

Also expect to see our living environment slowly but significantly redesigned to accommodate an aged population. To make life easier and more fulfilling, look for the following changes:

■ Larger typeface in books and magazines.
■ Traffic lights that change more slowly, giving pedestrians more time to cross streets, and senior drivers more time to respond.

- Buildings and malls using ramps and elevators, rather than stairs and escalators.
- More nutritious foods in grocery stores and restaurants.
- Carpeted, rather than waxed floors.
- Automobiles with larger mirrors, dashboards with fewer buttons and collision warning systems.
- More bathrooms with grab bars, seats built into the tub and temperature-sensitive water-heaters.
- Home storage areas that are more accessible.[4]

Another impact of our aging nation will be the heightened quest for companionship. Almost half of all adults 65 or older by 2000 will be single. This is partly due to increasing divorce rates among the elderly. By 2000, single elderly women will outnumber single elderly men by a 3.1 ratio.[5] Consequently, one of the traditions of American society—couples in which the male is older than the female—will begin to dissolve.

As Boomers Age

Notice that in 1996, Boomers will start to turn 50. As the Boomer generation enters its final decade before becoming senior citizens, Boomers will seek changes to pave the way for a comfortable and pleasurable transition into the final third of their lives. Perhaps the most fundamental transition that will occur will be a massive attitudinal shift.

For decades, Americans have held youth to be the prime time of life, the most pleasurable and cherished period of our existence. In the next two decades, Boomers will exhibit their well-worn tendency to characterize whatever they are experiencing to be both novel and of the utmost significance. As they enter their 50s and 60s, then, they will portray maturity as a time in which people can remain active, attractive, creative, future-oriented, healthy, productive, sexually involved and diverse in both interests and experiences.

✝ CHALLENGES AND OPPORTUNITIES FOR THE CHURCH

By the time 2000 arrives, the majority of the youth in America will be in their teens. That is our signal that the time is running short for reaching a substantial number of young people with the message of Jesus Christ.

Focus on Youth

Our surveys consistently show that more than two-thirds of all adults who have accepted Christ as their Savior made their decision to do so before the age of 18.[6] Obviously, the best time to reach them with the gospel is while they are young and impressionable, during the period in which they are solidifying their values and key attitudes. Time is rapidly running out for us to reach today's children and adolescents. We will not have such a large number of youths to evangelize for many years to come.

Since a majority of youth will be teenagers by the year 2000, we must begin to shift our resources from reaching children to reaching adolescents. Churches ought to be strategizing now for how this transition will take place. Facilities, equipment, teachers, curriculum and teaching resources will have to reflect the changing ages of the young people coming to the local church.

Another major shift affecting the Church is the reality that fewer and fewer adults will be visiting the Church as a result of the desire to see their children's spiritual needs addressed. During the late '80s and early '90s, millions of Boomers came back to church—mostly so their kids could receive some type of spiritual influence.[7] As their children age, and especially as they reach high school, family will be a less motivating factor for Boomers to visit and participate in churches. Again, time is of the essence, as the window of opportunity for reaching these marginally interested adults vanishes.

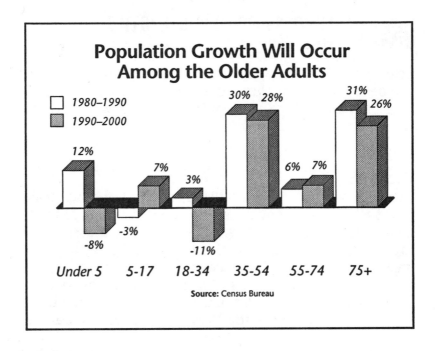

Focus on Seniors

We must begin to rethink ministry to older adults. The Church has been ministering to the elderly for many years. However, the new wave of elderly persons in the days ahead will be unlike the senior population of the past. As a first step toward effectively ministering to the new elderly, we must reshape our concept of what it means to be elderly, implanting a more positive vision of that age segment.

Programs at the Church must acknowledge that the senior citizens of tomorrow will be more physically vigorous, more interested in adventure and experiences and more involved in continuing education. Churches that treat older Americans as people who are simply winding down after an exhausting life, waiting to experience heaven, will find that their population of seniors will diminish steadily. Teaching, activities and programs will have to be reinvigorated to reflect the true needs and interests of our seniors.

A seminal shift in church ministry to the elderly will be the recognition that we will not be ministering simply to one segment of older people. Gerontologists tell us that come 2000, we might divide the elderly into three segments of mature adults: those age 50-64, those 65-79, and those 80 and older.[8] Not only will there be sufficient numbers of people in each group to justify such segmentation, but each group will have its own peculiar needs and expectations. Treating everyone who hits retirement age as though they were similar will no longer work.

Many churches will have to stop thinking of the elderly as a group to be ministered to, and see them as one of our most critical groups of lay ministers. Because we will have a senior population that is not seeking to sit back and observe life pass them by, it is imperative that churches recognize seniors' desire to be active participants in ministry, as in all other realms of their life.

Many churches may also have to reexamine policies regarding the retirement or phasing out of clergy. For thousands of churches, 65 is the magic age at which the shepherds of the flock are permanently put out to pasture. No longer will that perspective be valid. As we turn away from our emphasis on being young, and celebrate old age, leaders in all walks of life will be older than we have been accustomed to accepting.

Singles ministry, which came into its own during the '80s, will be even more important during the '90s and beyond. Churches must start to incorporate a senior singles ministry if the singles ministry is to be serving the needs of all of the unmarried adults in the church. With a large proportion of aging adults single, ignoring their needs would greatly undermine the value of a singles outreach. Among the tensions to be addressed in this regard will be the resistance to the separation of single seniors from their long-time senior friends who are still together.

Studies also indicate that tens of thousands of new churches will be planted during the '90s, and that tens of thousands of existing churches will rebuild or dramatically remodel their facilities. As buildings are developed, keep in mind the needs of older adults, designing the new structures with comfort and conveniences that will serve the needs of the elderly.

Notes
1. U. S. Census Bureau.
2. Ibid.
3. Den Dychtwald and Joe Fowler, *Age Wave* (Los Angeles: Tarcher, Inc., 1989), pp. 185-201.
4. Ibid., pp. 313-24.
5. U. S. Census Bureau.
6. From Omnipoll 1-89 and 6-88, studies conducted by Barna Research Group, Glendale, CA.
7. From studies conducted by Barna Research Group from 1986-1990.
8. Dychtwald and Fowler, op. cit., pp. 272-279.

13 BOOKS AND BUCKS: EDUCATION AND WEALTH

CHAPTER HIGHLIGHTS:

▶Significant educational changes are on the way: higher high school dropout rates and fewer people earning college degrees are likely; older adults are returning to colleges to update their skills.
▶The middle class will continue to shrink, resulting in an economically polarized society—the haves and the have-nots. Minorities and people in low-wage jobs will be particularly susceptible to economic decline.
▶Churches will have great opportunities to help promote literacy, to reach out to the poor and to help the affluent with estate planning.
▶Churches must also reassess the literacy level of the materials used in communicating the gospel.   ▶▶▶▶▶

THE RELATIONSHIP BETWEEN EDUCATION AND INCOME—NAMELY, THAT increased education leads to better jobs and higher income —has been widely accepted for several decades. Many parents convince their children to attend college by pointing to the economic benefits of a college education. As the demand for entry level employees escalates, the cost of a college education skyrockets, and wealth is redistributed, the '90s will redefine the correlation between levels of educational achievement and the accumulation of wealth.

AMERICA, 1990

Today, about one out of every five adults has earned a college degree. The proportion is somewhat higher among younger adults: about one in four people aged 25-44 (i.e., Baby Boomers) have completed college. The explosion of college degrees in the marketplace is a relatively recent phenomenon, however. Among the elderly, only one out of every ten has a college degree.[1]

While there is no denying that America has made great strides toward providing a more extensive education for a wide range of people, we are currently experiencing a barrier to continued growth in this area. Today, one of the most persistent problems confronting educators is our rising high school dropout rates. More than one out of every four people presently in high school will drop out before receiving a diploma.

The unwillingness to complete a standard high school education is a core reason why America today is struggling with the problem of functional illiteracy. Researchers estimate that America's functionally illiterate population—defined as people who cannot read and write at an eighth grade level—includes about 30 million people (although some estimates place that number as high as 60 million). One recent study stated that 61 percent of all 17-year-olds in the U.S. cannot read their high school textbooks.

Dropouts and Dollars

What about the tie between education and income? If we examine the median household income of Americans, it seems that the increasing failure of many Americans to complete at least a high school education has not yet impacted average income levels. Over the past several decades, the median income level has risen consistently. Today, the average household brings in just under $28,000, before paying Uncle Sam his share. We now have more than a million millionaires in this country, and the proportion of households who are making more than $75,000 has more than doubled in the past decade.

However, simply looking at median income levels can be misleading. The median has risen because of two major factors. First, inflation has raised household income levels. Second, we have millions of households who are increasing their annual income by double-digit margins. The magnitude of those increases has hidden the fact that we have concurrently had substantial growth in the number of households struggling to get by. Today, almost one out of every five households lives on an annual income of less than $10,000.[2]

The Polarization of Wealth

America is rapidly becoming a two-class nation: the haves and the have-nots. In relative terms, the rich *are* getting richer, while the poor *are* getting poorer. The American dream, based on living a comfortable, middle-class life, is in the process of being redefined, as the middle class shrinks into oblivion.

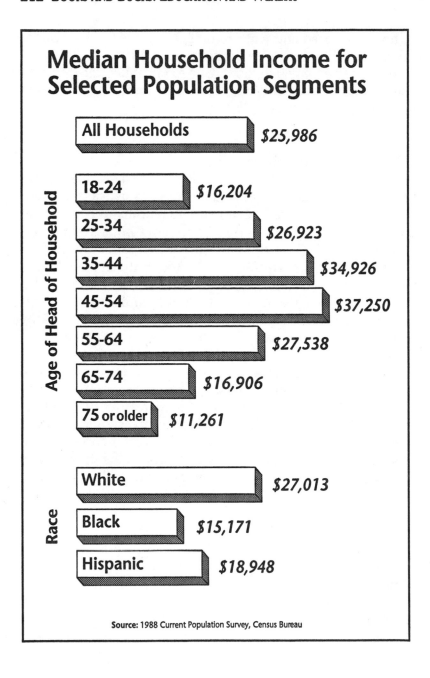

Median Household Income for Selected Population Segments

All Households — *$25,986*

Age of Head of Household

18-24 — *$16,204*

25-34 — *$26,923*

35-44 — *$34,926*

45-54 — *$37,250*

55-64 — *$27,538*

65-74 — *$16,906*

75 or older — *$11,261*

Race

White — *$27,013*

Black — *$15,171*

Hispanic — *$18,948*

Source: 1988 Current Population Survey, Census Bureau

Greater and greater proportions of the population are winding up at one or the other extreme of the income continuum. The richest 20 percent of the land are getting 44 percent of the nation's income, while the poorest 20 percent get less than 5 percent of the aggregate income.

Who Are the Poor?

Perhaps the saddest fact is that children are among the people most likely to suffer from poverty. Of all Americans living in poverty, 40 percent are children—about 13 million children. Studies estimate that we have more than 500,000 homeless children in America.[3]

We are also experiencing a shift in the demographics of poverty. In 1960, one out of every three people 65 and older lived in poverty. Today, just one in ten of our elderly are poor. Within the poor population, the fastest increase is among those who are working. Between 1986-1988, the proportion of poor people who were working rose 52 percent. During the same period, the proportion of poor who relied upon welfare for subsistence increased just 14 percent.[4]

Who controls the wealth? By and large, people who are 50 and older. Although this age group constitutes 25 percent of the population, they possess 70 percent of the nation's net worth; 77 percent of all financial assets; almost 50 percent of all discretionary income; and are responsible for 40 percent of all consumer spending. Obviously the dominance of the over-50 age group over the wealth in this nation is disproportional to their numbers.[5]

Race also has a strong impact on wealth. Although the majority of America is Caucasian, whites control a disproportionate amount of the country's wealth. For instance, the Census Bureau reports that among white households, the median annual income is nearly $28,780; among black households it is

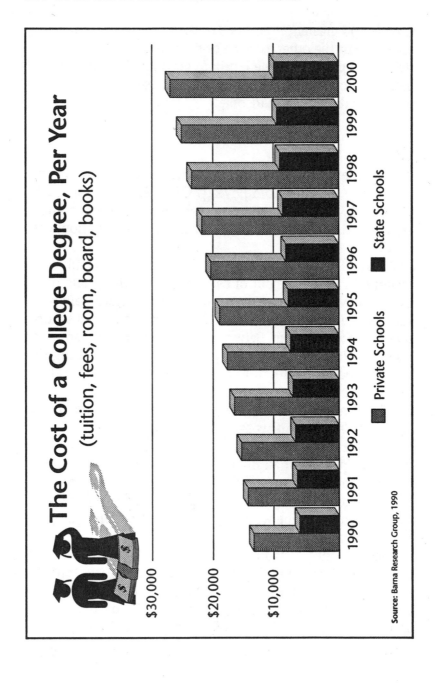

The Cost of a College Degree, Per Year
(tuition, fees, room, board, books)

Private Schools   State Schools

Source: Barna Research Group, 1990

barely half as much ($16,410). Hispanics do somewhat better ($20,360), but not much.[6]

 AMERICA, 2000

During the '90s, expect a continued increase in the proportion of people who leave school before earning a high school diploma. Part of this flight from the classroom will be due to the influx of Hispanic youths, millions of whom will not graduate. In addition, escalating divorce rates (and the resulting lack of family pressure to get an education), continued transience, tougher graduation requirements and the availability of unskilled jobs will make dropping out of school an attractive alternative to many.

Educational achievement will also be a function of a person's background. Of the four major racial groups in America, Asians are the most likely to graduate from high school and attend college. Hispanics and blacks graduate from high school at significantly lower rates. Currently, Hispanics are twice as likely as whites to drop out of school before graduating; blacks are 50 percent more likely than whites to drop out.

Higher Costs, Fewer Grads
In the coming decade we will notice a tailing off of the proportion of students who complete a college degree. About half of all whites who graduate from high school these days enroll in a college. However, only about one-third of them finish their college degree. One reason for this is the rapidly accelerating cost of a full, four-year college education.[7]

A student who graduates from a private college or university in 1990 after four years, will have spent an average of $51,000 (for tuition, room and board, books and fees) for a degree. That cost will double by the year 2000, when a degree earned from attending four years at a private institution will represent a $101,000 investment. Students wishing to receive a degree will be increasingly under pressure to either attend a state school, where the average four-year cost will be $40,000, or to apply for loans and grants.[8]

It will not be unusual for adults in their 30s, 40s and 50s to return to college and earn another degree, or a certificate in a specialized program.

Another popular course of action will be to graduate from high school and enroll in a two-year junior college. The number of students attending classes at such schools will increase by more than 15 percent by 2000, placing over 6 million students in such an academic setting. This will represent half of the aggregate college population.[9]

Junior colleges are attractive for a variety of reasons. Perhaps most important, they are less expensive than four-year institutions. Even students who plan to complete a four-year degree can realize savings of up to $60,000 by finishing their initial two years of study at a junior college. In addition, these schools have minimal entrance requirements; provide an opportunity to gain exposure to different disciplines without making a long-term commitment to education; and allow the student to live at home or nearby. Again, given the appeal of available entry-level positions, ending one's college career after a year or two of studies will become more common.

Second Career Students

At the same time, millions of adults, many of whom are already college-educated, and who have worked for years in an established career path, will decide to return to college. These adults will be seeking either to update their training or to prepare for an entirely new career. Career changes will be more common in the '90s and beyond, as the economy provides more service-sector jobs that utilize transferable skills. It will not be unusual for adults in their 30s, 40s, and even in their 50s to return to college and earn another degree, or a certificate in a specialized program.

Boomers, freed from child-rearing duties, bored with their current occupations and flush with discretionary dollars for the first time, will lead the charge back to the classroom. Their motivation will be the promise of conquering new and more attractive horizons: better financial opportunities, more exciting industries to operate within, a change of the day-to-day routine.

Unfortunately, simultaneous to this education-based campaign to realize upward mobility, it appears that we will also experience a widening of the gap between the rich and the poor. As the cost of living climbs, the proportion of working poor will also escalate. Minorities (mostly blacks and Hispanics) will bear the brunt of this ongoing hardship. Although the median household incomes of all age and racial groups will rise in the coming decade, it will rise more slowly than during the '80s; and the smallest increases will be among blacks and Hispanics.[10]

Baby Boomers will begin to reach the good life as their expenses level off and their incomes continue to rise The result will likely be greater discretionary income and personal savings. While the older population (those currently age 50 or older) will continue to control the bulk of the economic largess of America, Boomers will make dramatic strides toward financial independence and greater economic fulfillment. (However, they will never really be satisfied: studies suggest that even among those who are earning incomes that place them in the top 2 percent of the nation already, they do not feel that they are wealthy, nor that they have enough money on which to live comfortably.)[11]

✝ CHALLENGES AND OPPORTUNITIES FOR THE CHURCH

Local churches with a desire to minister to those in need will not fail to notice that the affluence of the nation at large will not be able to mask the dire poverty that will overcome a growing proportion of people in virtually every community. In addition to the homeless, we will have to contend with those who are functionally illiterate; minorities who, having shunned formal education, are also culturally illiterate (in American customs); and people who work steadily but are unable to make ends meet. These problems will be especially prevalent in our cities.

Pressure will grow for local churches to aid ethnic groups in gaining a more equitable share of wealth. As the Hispanic population in particular becomes an important segment of the work force, there will be battles over wage disparity and unequal benefits given to different classes of workers. The response of local churches will determine, for many observers, how serious we are about love, equality and justice.

Churches will have the opportunity to establish programs that address the needs that our formal educational system will no longer satisfy. Programs in basic language and mathematical skills will find a ready audience. Classes and counseling related to household finances will become more desirable as increasing numbers of people strain to survive on their incomes. Providing tangible resources and encouragement for those who lack basic skills and necessities will be a critical function of any "servant" church.

Tailoring Our Approach

In our attempts to reach out to people, we must reevaluate the materials used to communicate. As language skills deteriorate, our methods of communication must adapt to the abilities of the audience. Bulletins, newsletters and reports should have fewer words, and more pictures and symbols. Bible translations and hymnals must reflect the language skills of those using the materials. Written documents should require a minimal level of reading comprehension and writing ability if we wish to have widespread involvement.

Is this approach demeaning, insulting the intelligence of the people and simply perpetuating the problem? Not if it is in response to a population that is interested in the truth of the Bible and the claims of Jesus Christ, and who would otherwise be barred from exposure to those truths. While the Church has a responsibility to help people improve their life through social outreach, its primary responsibility is to touch people's lives with a spiritual message. This means communicating with people on a level with which they are capable and comfortable. Literacy programs can seek to raise skill levels. In the meantime, we dare not risk losing the interest and involvement of people simply because we have chosen to communicate over their heads.

A Higher Stake in Education

One of the negative implications of the growing school dropout rate is the prospect of declining enrollments in Sunday School classes. The increases in children's and adolescent Sunday School class enrollments that have occurred in the late '80s and which will continue in the early '90s will plateau in mid-decade, and tail off precipitously thereafter. As increasing numbers of teenagers make their own decisions about how to spend their time, they are likely to follow an established pattern: i.e., to decide that schooling and religion are two activities in which they have little interest. It becomes especially urgent, then, that we upgrade the quality of Sunday School programs so that our young adults will choose to attend because they feel it provides them such a valuable benefit.

Congregations may also wish to consider making community colleges a priority for ministry. There are more than 1,200 community colleges and junior colleges in the United States. Churches, however, generally avoid those campuses as outposts for ministry because the schools have a transient population that usually exhibits a minimal interest in religious matters. However, given the decreasing number of youth in our communities, focusing upon these campuses may provide a great opportunity to touch lives that would otherwise be missed.

Among the growing population of senior adults, there will be dramatically increased opportunities to help people with estate planning. Some churches have already developed programs in which the church assists people in creating wills and establishing living trusts. By working on planned giving, churches are often able to increase their potential revenue, as a preparation for the future.

Notes
1. Margaret Ambry, *1990-1991 Almanac of Consumer Markets* (Ithaca, NY: American Demographics Press, 1989), p. 105.
2. "1988 Current Popoulation Survey," Bureau of the Census, 1988.
3. Jonathan Kozol, "The New Untouchables," *Newsweek*, special issue Winter/Spring, 1990, pp. 48-49.
4. U. S. Census Bureau
5. Dychtwald and Fowler, *Age Wave*, p. 269.
6. American Demographics, July, 1989.
7. Ambry, op. cit., p. 55.
8. Barna Research Group projections, based on data provided by the U. S. Department of Education.
9. "America's Best Colleges—1990," *U.S. News and World Report*, special edition 1989, p. 37.
10. U. S. Census Bureau
11. From a study by Daniel Yankelovich, cited in *Advertising Age*, July 10, 1989, p. 55.

PART VI

A CHRISTIAN RESPONSE TO CHANGE

For the Christian community, the '90s will be a time of unprecedented challenge—and opportunity.

14 WANTED: CREATIVE RESPONSE TO A CHANGING WORLD

W HETHER OR NOT EACH OF THE PREDICTIONS ABOUT THE FUTURE contained in this book come true, one thing is certain: America will be substantially different in the year 2000. Unparalleled change will sweep the nation, and transform every dimension of life in this country.

For the Christian community, the '90s will be a time of unprecedented challenge—and opportunity. While many of the changes that will occur could threaten the stability and capacity of the Church to make an impact on our society, other changes are opening the doors for new forms of ministry.

Clearly, the Christian Body cannot hope to have much of an impact if we respond in the same ways we have in the past. These are new challenges, demanding creative, unique responses. The solutions that worked ten or even five years ago will fail in the coming decade. We are being confronted with a new wave of obstacles and opportunities. After careful study of our options, and discerning the mind of God, we must tailor new strategies to address this new environment.

Have we reached the end times, graphically described in the book of Revelation? Jesus Himself told His disciples that no one would know when the final days would be; not even He knew when they would come. Futurists and self-proclaimed prophets who claim that they have identified the date of the final times are fooling themselves, if nobody else.

But our inability to foretell the exact timing of the end of civilization should not deter us from our appointed responsibilities. Every Christian has been gifted in special ways to perform specific tasks for the kingdom of God. We are to work individually and corporately toward winning the world for Christ.

Nor should ignorance of the exact date of the coming judgment steal our passion for ministry, and our sense of urgency about serving God. We ought to act as if these are the final moments of time, and make the most of the chances we have to share truth and salvation with others.

During this decade, the Church will be pressured from all sides to give up the battle. The intensity of the spiritual warfare unraveling in our midst will accelerate. Each of us will find it tougher and tougher to muster the courage, the excitement and the energy to combat evil.

An evaluation of the behavior of the American Church over the past two decades surely indicates that one reason why we have had such a limited impact is that we have acted as a splintered Body, striving without vision and without a set of priorities for outreach. We cannot afford to make the same mistakes during the '90s.

During this decade, ministry will undergo dramatic changes, regardless of our response to our shifting surroundings. The Christian community must develop a new strategic approach for reaching America. We have to start from scratch and create a plan for ministry that acknowledges our new surroundings, obstacles, resources and opportunities. To be effective, it is imperative that we capture God's vision for ministry to America, and prepare a thoughtful plan that defines our priorities. We must then diligently pursue the completion of our plan, acting in ways which provide purpose for living, and hope for our nation.

DEVELOPING GOALS FOR MINISTRY

Throughout this book, ideas have been provided as to how the Church might respond to a rapidly changing world. More than a hundred potential responses are listed in the earlier pages. More ideas, in other words, than most individuals, groups or churches would feel capable of enacting.

The good news, however, is that because we are a community of believers, striving for the same outcome, we need not own each of those recommendations and assume the sole responsibility for seeing those ideas come to fruition. In fact, because we are a Body, the most rational strategy for effective ministry is for each of us—every individual and congregation—to identify the ministry gifts and resources available for responsive action, to tirelessly pursue their "short list" of challenges.

In the process of facing the future, however, the Christian Church must identify a series of goals that it wishes to satisfy during the coming decade. From the secular business world we can learn that organizations and movements which do not have clearly defined goals which result in measurable outcomes are unlikely to make the progress desired. We must create an agenda for action, mobilize our resources and move toward the fulfillment of our goals.

Naturally, if you put a dozen people seeking to serve God in a room and ask each one to identify the 10 most important goals for ministry, you will receive a dozen different plans for consideration. But that process of thinking through exactly what our priorities are, and what strategies are best for achieving the desired ends, is perhaps the first step that each Christian and each local church must take toward ensuring a Christian influence upon the nation.

Here, then, is my own list of 10 critical, achievable, goals that we, the Christian Body, might consider for the '90s.

1. Win People to Christ

Currently, 34 percent of the adult population claim Jesus Christ as their personal Savior. By 2000, we could reasonably raise that figure to 38 percent. This would add another 15 million adults to the body of believers. At a net gain of 1.5 million new believers per year, this is substantially more than we have been able to accomplish during the past three decades. These gains may be setting our sights short if we were to really take the Great Commission seriously. Even so, this modest growth rate will be difficult to achieve.

2. Raise Bible Knowledge

Few people read the Bible regularly, and even fewer know what is contained in the pages of Scripture. By 2000, we should strive to have the majority of all adults reading the Bible every day. We might seek to double the average amount of time spent reading the Bible per week (i.e., from one hour to two hours). We should set a goal of ensuring that most adults know why Jesus was sent to earth; the difference between the Christian faith and other faiths, and the meaning of, and means to salvation.

3. Equip the Christian Body

Part of the failure of today's church to reach the nation is the poor training we have provided for the Body of believers. Within the coming decade, we must refocus attention on the fundamentals of our faith. We must seek to have every believer regularly involved in a time of meaningful worship. We must encourage every believer to pray, and redefine "prayer ministry" to be a major underpinning of every individual and congregation. We need to turn around our churches, so that more money is given for outreach (domestic and international), and the focus of church ministry is not solely on the congregation, but on the community as well. And we must reintroduce the concept of spiritual accountability, ingraining discipling relationships among the majority of believers.

4. Establish Christian Community

A glaring weakness within today's Church is the lack of widespread relationships within, and the divisions between churches, denominations and parachurch ministries. While there may significant theological and methodological hurdles preventing the development of an ecumenical movement, the '90s must be a time when all people and organizations who love Jesus Christ and wish to serve Him put aside their differences, find their areas of commonality, and develop an agenda for powerful cooperative ministry within America. By 2000, perhaps we can create a unified movement of churches, organizations and individuals dedicated to restoring the Christian character of American society.

5. Renew Christian Behavior

To the average nonbeliever, Christians act no differently than anyone else. Our faith appears to be simply a theoretical construct, an emotional decision that does not have the power to transform who we are and how we behave. During the '90s, we must forcefully demonstrate, through our actions, that what we believe dictates what we do. We might strive to raise church attendance from the current 40 percent to 60 percent. We could seek to increase involvement in church leadership and volunteer activity to incorporate at least 25 percent of our people. Christians should be discernible as people of integrity and love. We must stand out as the people who sacrifice time and money to help the needy. Our decision-making should be overtly different because we are seeking to make choices that coincide with our faith.

6. Enhance the Image of the Local Church

People turn their back on the Church because they do not believe it is relevant, that it is personal, that the people of the Body care about outsiders or that it is concerned about the world. During the next decade, we have a great opportunity to reposition the Church and enhance that image. By acknowledging the state of the nation, and becoming involved in the thinking and activities that improve quality of life, we can redefine the relevance of the Church. By refining the thinking of Christians so that they see themselves as ministers of the gospel, and as 24-hour-a-day marketing agents for the Church, we can start to make the Church a more personal place. Church activities can be restructured to facilitate relationships. In an environment in which people are actively searching for institutions which promote a focus on people and the satisfaction of felt needs, we can make significant headway in improving the image of the local body.

7. Champion Christian Morals

Let's face it: if we do not stand up for Christian moral principles, nobody will. These are the principles we have been chosen to protect and disseminate. Yet, American society is dedicated to creating a new moral code. During the '90s, we can support leaders who articulate the Christian position and serve the cause of the Church in battling those who would institute a new moral and ethical tradition. Issues such as poverty, justice, discrimination, abortion and sexual promiscuity each present an opportunity for us to apply the gospel. Our past experience has shown that within our own communities we sometimes become hopelessly snared in the theological implications of these issues. If nothing else, however, we can elevate the discussion within the Church to the point at which Christians seriously attempt to apply their faith to the issues, and seek to make American society—the legislative, judicial and administrative ends of our government—responsive to a higher order of thought about these matters.

8. Live by a Christian Philosophy of Life

Most Americans live for the moment. By 2000, what a different country this would be if we could get a majority of adults to accept basic Christian principles and use those as the standard for their daily behavioral decisions. In the absence of a concerted effort to see a Christian philosophy of life adopted on a widespread basis, we can expect to see massive encroachment of materialism, syncretism and me-ism. Not only must the Church begin to teach people about the means to and the benefits of a Christian perspective toward life; we must model this approach to life.

9. Restore People's Self-esteem

America is besieged by a low sense of self-esteem. Rather than seeking quick fix solutions from pop psychologists, we ought to encourage people to seek their self-worth through Christ. Imagine the consequence if we could get people to understand that their value is not self-determined, but has already been determined for them by God. Along the way, if we can refocus attention upon the concept of love, making it a core element of our thoughts and a driving motivation behind our behavior, America would be a transformed nation. Ours would instantly become the most attractive nation on earth, causing Christianity to explode across the world.

10. Focus on Reaching the World for Christ

This goal is purposely listed last, not because it is least important but because the accomplishment of the preceding items would greatly facilitate worldwide evangelism by the Church in America. Again, the Great Commission must be taken seriously. It includes no geographic boundaries. Just as we have had to struggle with the development of relevant, practical and reasonable strategies for reaching America, we must take the time and devote the resources to doing the same in every other nation of the world.

Maybe you agree that these 10 elements represent the charge for the future for the American Church. Maybe you don't. The key is that you develop a prioritized plan for ministry, for yourself and for your church, and commit yourself to fulfilling that plan.

In an era of change and turbulence, as the '90s will be, there is little hope that the Church of Jesus Christ will make a difference unless each of us initiates an unbreakable covenant with God that we will serve Him with all of our heart, mind and soul, for His glory.

AN ALTERNATIVE DAY IN THE LIFE OF JILL: MAY 17, 2000

THE ALARM RUDELY AWOKE JILL AT 7 A.M. GROGGILY SLIDING OUT OF bed, she put on her housecoat and knocked on Jackson's door to get him going for his day at school. After a quick pit stop, she moved into the kitchen to prepare breakfast for both of them. Before launching into their food, they read a chapter of the Bible together and offered a short prayer about the approaching day. Between bites, they traded descriptions of what they anticipated the next 10 hours to hold in store. While Jackson went to brush his teeth and get ready for his walk to the bus stop, Jill got the money out of her purse for his lunch that day.

After kissing her son good-bye, she ran to the bedroom to get ready for her day at work. While her job was not the most fulfilling way to spend a day, she gave thanks to God every morning for providing a steady income and a respectable occupation. With the nation increasingly comprised of either rich or poor, she felt fortunate to have a job in which she was able to serve others in some capacity while earning a decent living.

On the way to work, she listened to the public radio station, and reflected on a special about social problems in America. It broke her heart to hear the stories about people who worked full time and still could not make enough to get by. In between accelerating and braking on the freeway, she again said a brief prayer of thanks for her own good fortune.

At work, she stopped at each computer work station to greet her fellow employees. Entering her own office, she switched on her machine and got involved in the tasks at hand. Only seven hours to get these tasks done. She'd give it her best shot before departing for the weekend.

At lunch time, she met a friend who worked in the same office complex for a sandwich at the complex snack shop. She and Pat, her lunch partner, met a couple times a week for lunch, to stay in contact and encourage each other. Pat, too, was a single mother with an adolescent at home.

They had met several months earlier at a seminar series sponsored by Pat's church, which was only a few blocks from Jill's home. Although Jill had not intended to explore the church, she was interested in the seminar topic—stress reduction for female managers—and she attended all four weekly sessions. She had met several people there with whom she had since remained in contact. Pat was one of those people.

Pat subsequently invited Jill to attend one of the church's Sunday services. Reluctantly—more out of loneliness than anything else—Jill did so. Pleasantly surprised, she returned the following week, and the week after that. After a couple of months of fairly regular attendance, she was invited to a home Bible study group. Again, driven by the desire to meet people of similar backgrounds, she attended and was pleased with the outcome. In fact, much of her social life now revolved around relationships with people she had met through that church. While Jill still found it difficult to make lasting friendships, at least she felt more connected than before she got involved with the church.

She was also pleased that Jackson attended the church with her one weekend, and found it "bearable"—his way of acknowledging that it was an acceptable place to spend an hour or two on Sundays. Now he occasionally accompanied her on Sundays.

Jill had been communicating with the central office of her company to pursue the possibility of instituting a flex-time policy for her branch. A central part of her argument was that the productivity rates would likely increase if the employees—who were mostly women with young or adolescent children at home—could work their schedules around their family needs. Jill had become somewhat of an advocate for parent-child relationships since the stress seminar had focused upon the importance of having stable and significant family relationships. She had already noticed the difference that spending more time with Jackson had made in their own lives.

She was looking forward to Friday evening. Jackson was on the school basketball team, and there was a 6 P.M. game at school. She planned to watch the game, root for Jackson and his team, then take him out for dinner afterwards. Just thinking about him, she again offered a silent prayer of thanks to God. At one of the recent basketball games she had the opportunity to speak with another player's mother, who was also waiting for her son to shower and dress after the game.

Although she had not seen that woman since, the conversation made a significant impact on Jill's thinking about her role as a parent. Without preaching at her, the other mother told of a turning point in her relationship with her son. Once anxious about how her son would respond to dangerous opportunities, she eventually "trusted God" to watch over her son. As Jill listened to the woman's story, she decided to try the same approach. She stopped worrying about the harmful influences Jackson might encounter, and realized that he was a good kid looking for her approval. Jill began to trust him and found that it enabled her to enjoy her relationship with her son much more.

Jill was looking forward to seeing Dan on Saturday night. A school teacher, Dan had also been divorced from his wife several years ago. He and Jill went out occasionally. It was upon his advice that Jill had started saving up for her son's college education. While she would probably not have the funds to send him to a top-flight private university, at least he could count on a degree from a four-year state college if she diligently saved during his remaining school years. Although it meant that she had to do without some of the luxuries she personally cherished—the latest styles in clothing, exotic meals, travel—it was a long-term investment she believed in.

During the day on Saturday, Jill regularly volunteered some time to help with a community elderly care program. Although her parents had died some years ago, Jill had felt increasingly troubled by the absence of quality care for the elderly. When a group of adults from the area began a community program to serve the elderly, Jill got involved. She had even taken Jackson with her on weekends when he was free. Everyone involved found the experience to be a good one. She had also found that she had much in common with a number of other people participating in the elder care work. A few good friendships had resulted.

Jill felt less exhausted these days. She had slowed down after recognizing that her upward-mobility and fragmented life-style were causing her to feel empty, both physically and emotionally. Her religious awakening was certainly helping to fill the void. But her decision to slow down had definitely been a major part of her heightened enjoyment of life. Previously, she was driven to control her world. Now, she was willing to trust that God had things under His control—and was undoubtedly more capable of managing her life than she was.

Things were looking up for Jill. She knew she would probably never have all the things she would have enjoyed owning, or visiting all the places in the world that she dreamed about. But it didn't seem to matter as much anymore. There were other considerations now: caring for Jackson, growing in her understanding of God and His son Jesus, experiencing new relationships with the other adults she was meeting through the church and some of her community activities.

People all around her continued to operate in the frenzy of activity that had formerly defined her own life. But she was beyond that now. As the world around her continued to change with each passing day and each technological break-through, she was more enthusiastic about leading a life of sim-plicity and wholesomeness. Life wasn't any less complex or demanding, but her perspective on her role in God's creation was changing. She was at peace with the world now, rather than trying to challenge and overwhelm it. What a difference a few friends with a different perspective about life had made!

For more information about George Barna and the work
of the Barna Research Group, please write:

Barna Research Group,
P.O. Box 4152,
Glendale, CA 91222-0152